SACRED SONGS OF INDIA

VOLUME TWO

Books by V.K. SUBRAMANIAN

The Holistic Way to Health, Happiness and Harmony

Sacred Songs of India — Volume I

Saundaryalahari

Maxims of Chanakya

Planets, Palms and Predictions

The Indian Financial System

Sivanandalahari

Rudraprasna

Portraits of Greatness

Lali and Other Short Stories

Love Twigs

A Bond to Sorrow

SACRED SONGS OF INDIA

VOLUME TWO

V.K. SUBRAMANIAN

ABHINAV PUBLICATIONS

abhinav publications

First Published in India 1998

Publishers

Shakti Malik
Abhinav Publications
E-37 Hauz Khas
New Delhi-110016, (INDIA)
Phones: 6566387, 6524658
Fax: 91-11-6857009
e-mail: shakti@nde.vsnl.net.in
abhinav.abhinaf@axcess.net.in

ISBN 81-7017-366-3

Phototypeset by

Tara Chand Sons
Naraina, New Delhi

Printed at

D.K. Fine Art Press P. Ltd.
Ashok Vihar, Delhi

To my brother
V.K. Sthanunathan
to whom I owe so much and have
repaid so little!

CONTENTS

ACKNOWLEDGEMENTS

I owe a non-repayable debt of gratitude to:

Sri R. Swaminathan, but for whose loving assistance rendered in writing out the songs in the Devanagari script and transliterating them into English, this book would not have been possible.

Mrs. Snehalata Datar who helped locate the right selections of songs of Jnaneshwar and Narsi Mehta and helped in their translation from Marathi and Gujarati into English.

Shrimati Arundhati Roy for selecting the songs of Rabindranath Tagore and suggesting the appropriate ragas for them.

Mrs. Premlata Chari and Sri Sitaram Sharma, Directors, Kalapeetham, and Sri V.A.K. Ranga Rao for helping in the translation of the songs of Annamacharya from Telugu to English.

Mrs. B. Jayalakshmi for help rendered in the translation of the Tamil songs of Subramania Bharati and Papanasam Sivan.

Chennai **V.K. Subramanian**

KEY TO TRANSLITERATION AND PRONUNCIATION

Devanagari letter	Transliterated as	Sounds like	Devanagari letter	Transliterated as	Sounds like
अ	a	o in son	ट	ṭ	t in ten
आ	ā or aa	a in master	ठ	ṭh	th in ant-hill
इ	i	i in if	ड	ḍ	d in den
ई	ī	ee in feel	ढ	ḍh	dh in child-hood
उ	u	u in full	ण	ṇ	n in under
ऊ	ū	oo in boot	त	t	t in French
ऋ	r	somewhat between r & ri	थ	th	th in thumb
ए	e	ay in May	ध	dh	th in breathe
ऐ	ai	y in my	न	n	n in not
ओ	o	o in oh	प	p	p in pen
औ	au	ow in now	फ	ph	ph in loop-hole
क	k	k in keen	ब	b	b in bag
ख	kh	ckh in black-head	भ	bh	bh in abhor
ग	g	g in go	म	m	m in mother
घ	gh	gh in log-hout	य	y	y in yard
ङ	ng	ng in singer	र	r	r in run
च	ch	ch in chart	ल	l	l in luck
छ	cch	ch in chain	व	v	v in avert
ज	j	j in judge	श	ś	ch in reich
झ	jh	dgeh in hedgehog	ष	sh	sh in show
ञ	n	n (somewhat) in French	स	s	s in sun
			ह	h	h in hot
			ळ	ḷ	ll in pull
			ऴ	zh	j in jean (French)

INTRODUCTION

This sequel to the first volume of the *Sacred Songs of India* has been prompted by the favourable response received by its predecessor.

The Sacred Songs of India, Volume Two, like volume one, encompasses selections from the lifework of ten mystic poet-musician-saints of India spanning twelve centuries. These poet-sages came from different regions of India and sang in different languages, but they were all mystics who sought and attained direct communication with God as the intangible, omniscient, omnipresent Power or in diverse manifestations of Divinity in personalised forms celebrated in the myths and legends of India.

As in volume one, the selection of sacred songs included in this volume is arbitrary, incomplete and whimsical.

Though God-intoxication is a running thread in the songs of this volume, as in the first, there are some differences I would like to highlight for the benefit of my readers.

The songs in the first volume focussed on one Deity: Krishna who is also Rama.

The songs in the present volume are hymns of praise to other manifestations of Divinity as well: like Siva, the Auspicious One, Sakti, the Divine Mother, Ganesa the darling deity and Kumara or Kartikeya or Subrahmanya, the embodiment of youth and beauty and valour, the favourite Deity in most of Tamil Nadu. God is also addressed in the abstract by poet-singers like Rabindranath Tagore.

The mystic poets, whose songs are included in this volume, are:

Manikkavachakar, the Saivite saint who lived earlier than the 9th century A.D.

Jnaneshwar, the famous Maharashtra saint who lived in the 13th century A.D. (1275-1296 A.D.)

Narsi Mehta, the saint from Gujarat who lived in the 15th century (1414-1480 A.D.)

Annamacharya, the Telugu saint-poet who also lived in the 15th century (1424-1503 A.D.)

Syama Sastri, one of the Trinity of Carnatic music (1762-1827 A.D.)

Muthuswami Dikshitar, the Tamil music composer, a contemporary of Syama Sastri and also one of the Trinity of Carnatic music (1775-1835 A.D.)

Swati Tirunal, the Maharaja of Travancore, who lived in the 19th century (1813-1846 A.D.)

Rabindranath Tagore, the great Nobel-Laureate, who belongs to the 20th century (1861-1941 A.D.)

Subramania Bharati, a contemporary of Tagore, who, apart from being a great patriot, was also a mystic poet who sang of the glories of his beloved Deities (1882-1921 A.D.)

Papanasam Sivan, the South Indian composer who was very much a 20th century Tamil musical icon (1890-1973 A.D.)

The songs of Manikkavachakar are soaked in bridal mysticism, as those of Andal, presented in the first volume, though the Deities idolised are different.

The approach of Jnaneshwar, who lived in the 13th century, towards the universe as a joyful expression of God is the same as that of Rabindranath Tagore and Subramania Bharati of the 20th century.

The various temples of India provided the inspiration for the songs of Manikkavachakar, Jnaneshwar, Annamacharya, Syama Sastri, Muthuswami Dikshitar, Swati Tirunal, and Papanasam Sivan. The songs of Narsi Mehta are the culmination of the Bhakti movement which started in the 7th century in South India, with the Alwars and Nayanars.

Manikkavachakar, Subramania Bharati and Papanasam Sivan sang in Tamil, Muthuswami Dikshitar and Swati Tirunal in Sanskrit, Syama Sastri and Annamacharya in Telugu, Jnaneshwar in Marathi, Narsi Mehta in Gujarati and Rabindranath Tagore in Bengali.

These diverse musical compositions imbued with God-intoxication and mysticism are presented on a common platter, in a common language to be savoured by people all over the world, irrespective of their religion, race, language or nationality.

Listening to these marvellous songs set in melodious tunes is a spiritual experience that enthralls and elevates everyone.

Chennai **V.K. Subramanian**

SONGS OF MANIKKAVACHAKAR

(9th Century A.D.)

	Song	*Rāga*
	(Tiruvembavai)	
1.	Aatiyum antamum	Bhoopalam
2.	Paasam paramjothi	Kedaram
3.	Muthanna	Bilahari
4.	Onnithilanagaiyaai	Devagandhaari
5.	Maalariyaa naanmukhanum	Yadukula Kambodhi
6.	Maane nee	Khamas
7.	Anne lvayum	Ritigowla
8.	Kozhi chilamba	Dhanyasi
9.	Munnaippazhamporutku	Saurashtra
10.	Paataalam	Suddha Saveri
11.	Moyyaar	Poorvikalyani
12.	Aartha piravi	Sankarabharanam
13.	Painkuvalai	Saveri
14.	Kaataar Kuzhaiyaada	Suddhadhanyasi
15.	Ororukaal	Huseni
16.	Munnikkadalai	Amritavarshini
17.	Senkanavanpaal	Vasanta Bhairavi
18.	Annamalaiyaan	Sama
19.	Ungaiyirpillai	Vasanta
20.	Potri aruluka	Madhyamavati
	(Tiruppalliyezhucchi)	
21.	Potri yen	Bhoopalam
22.	Arunan Indiran	Kedaram
23.	Koovina poonguyil	Bilahari
24.	Innisai	Devagandhari
25.	Bhootangal thorum	Yadukulakambodhi
26.	Papparaveettirunthu	Khamas
27.	Athu pazhacchuvai	Ritigowla
28.	Munthiyamuthal	Dhanyasi
29.	Vinnaga thevarum	Saurashtra
30.	Bhuvaniyir	Madhyamavati

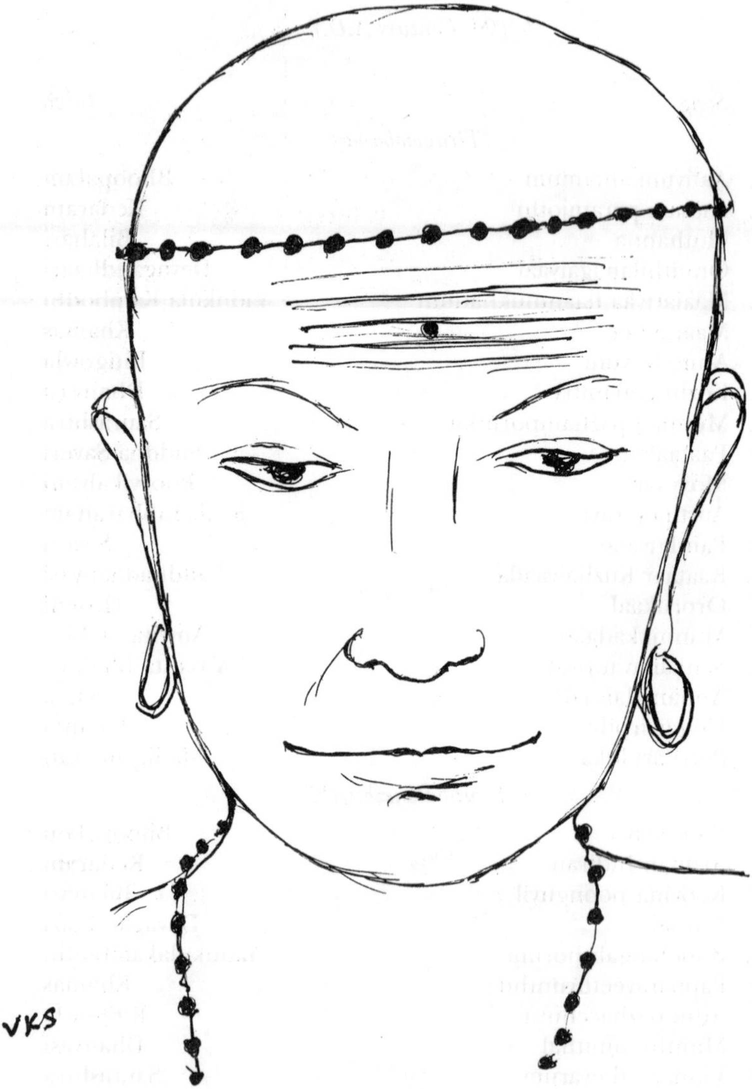

MANIKAVACHAKAR

MANIKKAVACHAKAR (9th Century A.D.)

The songs of Manikkavachakar, the Saivite saint, who is believed to have lived in the 9th century A.D., are imbued with bridal mysticism, like the songs of Andal, the Vaishnavite saint of the 7th century.

Manikkavachakar was born in *Tiruvadavur,* a place near Madurai, the Pandyan capital and his original name was *Tiruvadavurar.* He was devoted to Lord Siva from childhood and poured forth his devotion in mellifluous poetry and acquired the title of *Manikkavachakar* (lit.: "He whose words are rubies").

This South Indian saint has been compared to St. Augustine, St. Paul and St. Francis of Assissi.

The Lord was the object of his love and he deemed himself as the separated lover yearning for union with his love. Manikkavachakar's major works are the *Tiruvāchakam* and *Tirukkovaiyar,* the first comprising 656 verses and the latter 400 verses.

Among the various places of pilgrimage visited by Manikkavachakar, three temples are most important. These are the temple of *Tirupperundurai,* where he first perceived God as his teacher and composed the famous hymn: *Tiruppalliyezhucchi,* the temple of *Tiruvannamalai,* where he composed the *Tiruvembavai,* eulogising group worship by young girls during the month of Mārgasirsa (mid December to mid January), and the famous temple of *Chidambaram,* where he composed the *Tiruvāchakam* and attained salvation.*

The thirty songs of Manikkavachakar included in this book comprise: the *Tiruvembavai* (20 songs) and *Tiruppalliyezhucchi* (10 songs).

All these songs reveal intense devotion to God and self-surrender. In the eloquent words of Rev. G.U. Pope, "South India needed a personal God, an assurance of immortality and a call to prayer. These it found in Manikkavachakar's compositions."

*While the location of *Tiruvannamalai* and *Chidambaram* are wellknown, not many know where *Tirupperundurai* is located. This is because it is now known as *Aavudaiyaar Koil.* The location is in the *Arantaangi* taluq of Thanjavur district in Tamil Nadu. It is nine miles by road from Arantaangi railway station on the *Tiruvarur-Karaikudi* rail line. One can also drive from *Kāraikkudi.*

राग : भूपालं Rāga : Bhoopālam

1. आदियुं अन्तमुं इल्ला अरुं पेरुं
शोतियैयां पाटक्केट्टेयुं वाळ् तडंकण्
माते! वळरुतियो? वन्चेवियो निन् चेवितान्?
मादेवन् वार्कऴ्ऴल्कल् वाऴ्त्तिय वाऴ्त्तु ओलि पोय्
वीति वाय्कुकेट्टलमे, विम्मि विम्मि मेय्म्मरन्तु,
पोतु आर् अमलियिन्मेल् निन्रुं पुरण्डु, ईङ्गन्
येतेनुं आकाळ्, किटन्ताळ् ; येन्ने! येन्ने!
ईते यें तोऴि परिशु? - येल् ओरेंपावाय्

Ātiyum antamum illā arum perum
Śotiyaiyām pāḍakkéṭṭéyum vāḷ taḍam kaṇ
Māté! Vaḷarutiyo! Vancheviyo nin chevitan?
Mādevan Vārkazhalkal vāzhttiya vazhttu oli poy
Vīti Vāikkéṭṭalumé, vimmi vimmi meymmarandu
Pōtu ār amaliyin mél ninrum purandu ingan
Yéténum ākāḷ kiḍantāl yénné! yénné!
Ītē ém tózhi pariśu? - yél ór yémpāvāi

1. Aatiyum antamum

O! Beautiful girl, whose eyes resemble the wide sword!

Are you still asleep, despite hearing us sing of the Lord who has no beginning and no end and who is the embodiment of great effulgence?

Have your ears lost their power of hearing?

Hearing us sing of the lotus feet of the Great Lord, one girl sobbed in blissful ecstasy and, rolling in bed, became unconscious!

But you still do not wake up and continue to slumber. What is this? Wake up and come!

राग : केदारं Rāga : Kedāram

2. पाशं परं शोतिक्कु येन् पाय, इराप्पकल् नाम्
पेशुंपोतु: येप्पोतु इप्पोतु आर् अमळिक्के
नेशमुं वैत्तनैयो? नेरिऴैयाय्! नेरिऴैयीर्!
ची! ची! इवैयुं शिलवो? विळैयाटि
येशुं इटं ईतो? विण्णोर्कल् येत्तुतर्कुक्
कूशुं मलर्प्पातं तन्तरुळ वन्तरुळुम्
देशन्, शिव लोकन्, तिल्लैच्चिट्रंपलत्तुळ्
ईशनार्क्कु अन्पु आर्? यां आर्? येल् ओर् येंपावाय्

Pāśam param śotikku yénpāya irāppakal nām
Péśum pótu: yeppótu ippótu ár amalikké
Néśamum Vaittanayó? Nérizhaiyay! Nerizhaiyīr!
Chi! chi! ivaiyum śilavó? Vilaiyāti
Yéśum iṭam īdo? viṇṇorkal yéttudaṛkuk
Kūśum malavppādam tandarula vandaruḷum
Déśan Śivalokan tillaichchiṭrampalattul.
Īśanārkku anpu ār? yām ār? yél ór yémpāvāi

2. Pasam paramjothi

"All my love is for the Lord", you say whenever we talk and gossip; but now you seem to be more fond of your bed, You girl wearing precious ornaments!

"These are mere words! Is this the time and place for slander and derogatory talk?"

The Lord has appeared in holy Chidambaram to present His lotus feet for worship by the angels. Let us sing His praises!

राग : बिलहरि Rāga : Bilahari

3. मुत्तन्नवेण्णगैयाय ! मुन्वन्तु येतिर् येलुन्तु, येन्
अत्तन्, आनन्दन्, अमुतन् येन्रु अळ्ळूरित्
तित्तिक्कप्पेशुवाय्, वन्तु उन्कटै तिर्वाय्-
पत्तु उटैयीर् ! ईशन्पल् अटियीर् ! पाङ्कु उटैयीर् !
पु त्तु अटियोम् पुन्मै तीर्त्तु आट्कोण्टाल पोल्लातो ?
येत्तो निन् अन्पुटैमै ? येल्लों अरियोमो
चित्तं अलकियार् पाटारो, नं शिवनै ?
इत्तनैयुं वेण्डुं येमक्कु – येल ओर् येंपावाय्

Muttannavénnagaiyāy! munvantu yetir yezhuntu yen
Attan, Ānandan, amutan yénṛu aḷḷūrit
Tittikkappéśuvāi, vantu un katai tiṛavāi-
Pattu utaiyīr! īśānpaḷa aṭiyīr pānku uṭaiyīr!
Puttu aṭiyom punmai tīrttu ātkoṇṭāl pollāto?
Yétto nin anpuṭaimai? yellom aṛiyómā?
"Chittam aḷakiyār pāṭāro, nam Śivanai?"
"Ittānaiyum véṇtum émakku" - yél ór émpāvāi

3. Muthanna

You girl!, who smile, showing your pearlwhite teeth! You used to get up before us and speak honeyed words that "the Lord is the Father, He is the embodiment of bliss and ambrosia." But today you are still sleeping. Open the door!

"You are all sincerely devoted to the Lord, experienced in your love and devotion. I am comparatively new. You could have forgiven my fault. You only say in words you love me. Otherwise you could have shown me the right path."

"We know that your love is not untrue, people like you whose hearts are pure will not stay without singing about our Lord. That is why we invite you. This is what we need."

राग : देवगान्धारी Rāga : Devagāndhāri

4. ओन्नित्तिल नकैयाय्! इन्नं पुलर्न्दिन्नो?
वण्णक्किळि मोऴियर् येल्लारुं वन्दारो?
येण्णिक्कोटु उळ्ळवा शोल्लुकों अव्वळवुम्
कण्णैत्तुयिन्रु, अवमे कालत्तैप्पोक्काते
विण्णुक्कु ओरु मरुन्दै वेद विऴुप्पोरुळै
कण्णुक्कु इनियानै, पाडिककशिन्तु, उळ्ळं
'उळ्नेक्कु, निन्रु उरुग, यां माट्टों; नीये वन्तु
येण्णि, कुरैयिल, तुयिल् - येल् ओर् येंपावाय्

Onnittila nakaiyāy! innam pularndinro?
Vaṇṇakkiḷi mozhiyar yellārum Vandāro?
Yeṇṇikkoṭu uḷḷavā śollukóm avvaḷavum
Kaṇṇaittuyinṛu avamé kālattaip pókkāté
Viṇṇukku oru marundai Véda vizhupporulai
Kaṇṇukku iniyānai, pāḍikkaśindu uḷḷam
Uḷnekku, ninṛu uruga, yām māttóm, nīye vantu
Yeṇṇi kuṛaiyil, tuyil - yél ór émpāvāi

4. Onnithilanagaiyaai

"Is it not yet dawn for you, O! Girl with the lustrous pearlwhite smile?"

"Have all our friends, who speak sweetly like beautiful birds come?"

" We have counted and tell you: All have come. Should we not sing heartrendingly of the Lord who is like nectar to the angels, the Supreme Being eulogised by the Vedas, and beautiful to behold? Hence don't waste your time in sleep. If need be, come and count. If there is any shortage in attendance, you can go back and sleep!"

राग : यदुकुल काम्बोधि Rāga : Yadukula Kāmbodhi

5. मालऱिया नान्मुखनुं काणा, मलैयिनै, नाम्
पोल् अरिवों, येन्रु उळ्ळ पोक्कङ्कळे पेशुम्
पाल् ऊरुतेन् वाय्प्पटिऱी ! कटै तिऱवाय्,
ज्ञालमे, विण्णे, पिऱवे अऱिवु-अऱियान्
कोलमुं, नंमै आट्कोण्टु अरुळिक् कोताट्टुम्
शीलमुं पाटि, "शिवने, शिवने"! येन्रु
ओलं इटिनुं, उणराय्, उणराय् काण्!
येलक्कुऴलि परिशु – येल् ओर् येंपावाय्

Mālaṛiyā nānmukhanum Kāṇā Malaiyainai nām
Pól aṛivóm yenṛa uḷḷa pokkankale pesum
Pāl ūṛutén vāippaṭiṛī! kaṭai tiravāi
Jnālamé viṇṇé piṛave aṛivu-ariyān
Kólamum, nammai āṭkoṇṭu, aruḷikkotāṭṭūm
Śīlamum pāṭi "śivane śivane" yenṛu
Olam iṭinum, uṇarāi uṇarāi kāṇ!
Élakkuzhali pariśu - yél or yémpāvāi

5. Maalariyaa naanmukhanum

You deceiver whose words drip in milk and honey and falsely claim that you have understood the Great Lord, who could not be known or found by Vishnu and Brahma. Open the door!

You have not yet got up, despite hearing us sing of the greatness and protective compassion of the Lord who is so rare to be known in all these worlds of heaven and earth and call Him: "O! Siva, O! Auspicious One!"

Wake up and come! O girl with the sweetsmelling hair!

राग : खमाज़ Rāga : Khamās

6. माने नी नेन्नलै, नाळै वन्दु उङ्कळै
नाने येलुप्पुवन् येन्नालुं, नाणामे
पोन तिशै पकराय, इन्नं पुलर्न्तिन्रो ?
वाने, निलने पिऱवे, अऱिवु–अरियान्
ताने वन्दु, येम्मैत्तलैयाळित्तु, आट्कोण्डरुळुम्
वान् वार् कऴ़ल् पाटि वन्दोर्क्कु, उन वाय् निरवाय् !
ऊने उरुकाय्, उनक्के उरुं ; येमक्कुं
येनोर्क्कुं तं कोनैप्पाटु – येल् ओर् येंपावाय् !

Māne nī nennalai, nāḷai vandu ungkalai
Nāne yexhuppuvan yennāḷum nāṇāme
Pona tiśaipakarāi, innam pularntinro
Vāne, nilane piraue, aṛivu ariyān
Tāne vandu yemmait talaiyaḷittu, ātkonḍarulum
Vān vār kazhal pāṭi vandorkku, un vāi tiravāi
Une urukāi, unakke uṛum; yemakkum
Enorkkum tam konaippātu - yel or empāvāi

6. Maane nee

O! gazelle-like girl! You told us yesterday that you would come and wake us up. Where have those words gone with the wind?

It is not yet dawn for you!

Lord Siva, who cannot be realised by angels, humans or others has come on His own accord to us.

You have not opened your door to us who have come singing of His lotus feet.

Is this right on your part?

Come and sing joyously with us about the Lord who is not only our Master but also yours.

राग : रीतिगौल

Rāga : Rītigowla

7. अन्ने इवैयुं शिलवो ? पल अमरर्
उन्नर्क्कु अरियान्, ओरुवन् इरुंशीरान्,
चिन्नङ्गळ् केट्प, "शिवन्" येन्रेवाय् तिरप्पाय्
तेन्ना येन्नामुन्नं तीशेर् मेलुगु ओप्पाय्:
येन्नानै, येन् अरैयन्, इन् अमुतु, येन्नु येल्लोमुम्
शोन्नों केळ्, वेव्वेराय्; इन्नं तुयिलुतियो ?
वन् नेञ्जप्पेतैयर् पोल, वाळाकिटत्तियाल्
येन्ने तुयिलिन् परिशु - येल ओर् येंपावाय्

Anne ivaiyum śilavo? Pala amarar
Unnaṛkku aviyān, oruvan irum śīran,
Cinnangal ketpa śivan yenrévai tiṛappai
Tenna yennamunnan tīśér mezhugu oppai
Yennānai, yen araiyan in amudu yenru yellomum
Śonnom keḷ vevverāi; innam tuyilutiyo
Van nenjappedaiyaṛ pol vālākiṭattiyāl
Yenné tuyilin pariśu - yél ór yempāvāi

7. Anne Ivayum

Dear one! what is all this playfulness? When Lord Siva, who is hardly discernible by many of the angels and is of peerless fame, comes, auspicious signals sound and, hearing them, you would say "Siva! Siva!" and open the door.

Even before finishing the chantings of his Holy name, you would melt like wax and pine for Him!

Now, we are singing in invocation several times that "He is my Lord, my Kin, the sweet Ambrosial One etc." But you are not coming out and continue to sleep.

You sit still like the hard hearted foolish girls. What is the power of your slumber?

राग : धन्यासी Rāga : Dhanyāsi

8. कोऴि शिलंब, शिलुंबुं कुरुकु येङ्गुम्
येऴिल् इयंब इयंबुं वेण् शङ्गु येङ्गुम्;
केऴ् इल् परञ्चोति, केऴ् इल् परंकरुणै
केऴ् इल् विऴुप्पोरुळ्कळ् पाडिनों; केट्टिलैयो ?
वाऴि! ईनु येन्न उऱक्कमो ? वाय् तिऱवाय्!
आऴियान् अन्पुटमै आं आऱुं इव्वारो ?
ऊऴि मुतल्वनाय् निन्र ओरुवनै,
येऴै पङ्गाळनैये पाडु - येल् ओर् येंपावाय्!

Kozhi śilamba, śilumbum karuku yéngum
Yezhil iyamba iyambum véṇ śangu yengum;
Kezh il paranchoti, kéḷ il parankaruṇai
Kezh il vizhupporuḷkaḷ pādinōm; kéttilaiyo?
Vāzhi ītu yenna uṛakkamo? vāi tiṛvavāi!
Āzhiyān anbudaimai ām āṛum ivvāro?
Ūzhi mutalvanāi ninra oruvanai,
Yézhai pangālanaiye pādu - yel or yémpavāi!

8. Kozhi silamba

The cocks and other birds are crowing. Musical sounds are resonating. White conches are blowing loud.

Don't you hear us singing the glories of Lord Siva, the Resplendent One with infinite compassion?

What is this sleep? Open the door! May you live long. Probably even Vishnu worshipped Lord Siva sleeping in the ambrosial ocean.

Come, let us sing of the Lord who is deathless even in times of deluge!

राग : सौराष्ट्र Rāga : Saurāshtra

9. मुन्नैप्पऴं पोरुट्कुं मुन्नैप्पऴं पोरुळे!
पिन्नैप्पुतुमैक्कुं पेर्त्तुं अप्पेट्रियने
उन्नैप्पिरानाकप्पेट्र उन शीर् अटियोम्
उन् अटियार् ताळ् पणिवोम्; आङ्गु अवर्क्के पाङ्गु आवोम्;
अन्नवरे यें कणवर् आवार्; अवर् उकन्दु
शोन्न परिशे तोलुंपाय् प्पणि शेय्वोम्;
इन्नवकैये मेमक्कु येंकोन् नल्कुतियेल्,
येन्न कुरैयुं इलोम् – येल् ओर येंपावाय्

Munnaippazham porutkum munnaippazham porule!
Pinnaiputumaikkum pérttum appeṭriyané
Unnaippirānākappeṭra un śīr aṭiyom
Un aṭiyār tāḷ paṇivom; āngu avarkke pāngu āvom
Annavare yem kaṇavar āvār; avar ukandu
Śonna pariśé tozhumpāippaṇi śeivóm;
Innavakaiye yemakku yémkón malkutiyél,
Yenna kuṛaiyum ilóm - yél ór yempāvāi

9. Munnaippazhamporutku

O! Lord! You are the Primordial One, Ancient of all ancients!
You are also the newest of new, giving life to the youngest!
We are proud of worshipping you as our Lord!
We prostrate before your Holy Feet.
Your feet would be our companions, our husbands!
We will obey them and serve them.
If we get this blessing we do not need anything more.

राग : शुद्ध सावेरी Rāga : Suddha Sāveri

10. पाताळं येऴिनुं कीऴ् शोल–काऴिवु पादमलर्;
पोदु आर्पुनैमुडियुं येल्लाप्पोरुळ् मुडिवे!
पेदै ओरु पाल तिरुमेनि ओन्रु अल्लन्;
वेद मुदल विण्णोरुं मण्णुं, तुदित्तालुं,
ओद उलवा ओरु तोऴन् तोण्डर् उळन्
कोदु इल् कुलत्तु, अरन्–तन्कोयिल् पिनाप्पिळ्ळैकाळ्!
येदु अवन् ऊर्? येदु अवन् पेर्? आर् उट्रार् आर् अयलार्
येदु अवनैप्पाडुं परिशु? येल् ओर् येंपावाय्

Pātāḷam yézhinum kizh śol-kazhivu pādamalar;
Pódu ār punaimudiyum yellaporuḷ mudive!
Pédai oru pāl tirumeni onṛu allan;
Veda mudal viṇṇorum, maṇṇum, tudittālum,
Oda ulavā oru tozhan tonḍar uḷan
Kodu il kulattu, aran-tan koil pināppiḷḷaīgāl
Yedu avan ūr? yedu avan pér? ār utrar? ār ayalār?
Yédu avanaippādum pariśu? yél ór yémpāvāi

10. Paataalam

His lotus feet transcend the seven netherworlds and shine with indescribable splendour.

His crescent crested crown is the endgoal of all beings. His body is inseparable from the goddess: the Divine Mother. The Vedas proclaim Him as the Primordial One! But he is beyond all the scriptures.

His greatness is beyond the praises of angels and humans. And yet He lives in the innermost hearts of His devotees. O! Girls from faultless families who work and serve in His places of worship and have the opportunity of ever being with Him, please tell us: What is His hometown? What is His name? Who are His friends and relatives? Who are His neighbours? How can we sing and praise Him?

राग : पूर्वीकल्याणी Rāga : Poorvikalyāni

11. मोय्यार्तडं पोय्गै पुक्कु, मुकेर् येन्नक्
कैयाल् कुडैन्दु, कुडैन्दु, उन्कऴल् पाडि,
ऐया! वऴि अडियों वाऴ्न्दों काण् आर् अऴल्पोल
शेय्या! वेळ्नीरु आडि! शेल्वा! शिरु मरुङ्गुऴल्
मै आर् तडंकण् मडन्तै मणवाळा!
ऐया नी आट्कोण्डरुळुं विळैयाट्टिल्
उय्वार्कळ् उय्युं वगै येल्लां उय्न्दु ओऴिन्दोम्,
येय्यामल् काप्पाय् येमै – येल् ओर् येंपावाय्

Moyyārtaḍam poigai pukku, mukér yennak
Kaiyāl kuḍaindu, kuḍaindu un kazhal pāḍi,
Aiyā! Vazhi adiyóm vāzhndóm kāṇ ār azhalpol
Śeyyā! veḷnīṛu ādi! śelva! śiṛu marunguzhal
Mai ār taḍamkaṇ maḍantai maṇavāḷā!
Aiyā! nī āṭkoṇdaruḷum viḷaiyāṭṭil
Uyvārkaḷ uyyum vagai yellām uyndu ozhindóm
Yeyyāmal kāppāi yemai - yél ór yempāvāi

11. Moyyaar

We have lived for generations as your servants singing of your lotus feet bathing in the waters of the wide pond filled with beautiful flowers besieged by swarms of bees. O! Lord whose body is crimson like burning fire! O! Lord who wear the holy ashes! O! Treasurehouse of grace!

O! Lord of Uma, who has a small waist and large colloryed eyes! My Master! We have also undoubtedly attained salvation in your sports ruling all lives. Please protect us and bless that we continue unabated in your worship!

राग: शंकराभरणं Rāga : Sankarābharanam

12. आर्त्त पिऱवित्तुयर्केड, नां आर्त्तु आडुम्
तीर्त्तन्, नल् तिल्लैच्चिट्रंबलत्ते ती आडुम्
कूत्तन्, इव्वानुं, कुवलयमुं येल्लोमुं
कात्तुं, पडैत्तुं, करन्दुं, विळैयाडि,
वात्तैयुं पेशि, वळै शिलंब, वार्कलैकळ
आर्प्पुं अरवं शेय्य, अणिकुऴल मेल्वण्डु आर्प्प
पूत्तिकऴ्, पोय्गै कुडैन्दु, उडैयान् पोनपादम्
येत्ति, इरुं शुनै नीर् आडु - येल् ओर् येंपावाय्!

Ārtta piravittuyarkeda, nām ārtta ādum
Tīrttan, nal tillaichchitrambalatté tī ādum
Kūttan, ivvānum, kuvalayamum yellāmum
Kāttum, padaittum, karandum, viḷaiyāḍi
Vārttaiyum péśi, vaḷai silamba, vārkalaikaḷ
Ārppum aravam śeyya, aṇikuzhal melvaṇḍu ārppa
Pūttikazhum poyyai kuḍaindu, uḍaiyān ponpādam
Yētti, irumśunai nīrāḍu - yélóryempavāi!

12. Aartha piravi

Let us bathe joyously entering the lakes filled with flowers our hair mobbed by humming bees, our bangles jingling merrily and sing of the glories of Lord Siva who acts as the pond for us to bathe and destroy all our sorrows arising from our human birth, who dances holding fire in beautiful Chidambaram, and who engages in the divine sport of creating, protecting and destroying all this universe!

राग : सावेरी Rāga : Sāverī

13. पैं कुक्ळैक्कार् मलराल्, चेंकमलप्पैं पोदलाल्,
अङ्गं कुरुकु इनत्ताल्, पिन्नुं अरवत्ताल्,
तंकळ् मलं कलुवुवार वन्दु शार्दलिनाल्,
येङ्गळ् पिराट्टियुं यें कोनुं, पोन्रु इशैन्द
पोङ्ग मडुविल, पुगप्पायन्दु, पायन्दु; नम्
शङ्गं शिलंब, शिलंबु कलन्दु आर्प्प,
कोङ्गैगळ पोङ्ग, कुडैयुं पुनल् पोङ्ग,
पङ्गयप्पुनल् पायन्दु आडु - येल् ओर येंपावाय

Paim kuvalaikkār malarāl, chemkamalappaim pódalāl
Angam kuruku inattāl, pinnum aravattāl
Tankal malam Kazhuvuvār vandu śārdalināl,
Yengal pirāttiyum yem kónum ponṛu iśainda
Pongu maḍuvil pugappāindu, pāindu; nam
Śangam śilamba, śilamba kalandu ārppa
Kongaigaḷ ponga, kudaiyum punal ponga,
Pangayappūm punal pāindu āḍu - yél or yempāvāi

13. Painkuvalai

This pond is filled with blue lilies and red lotuses; lovely waterbirds chirp, snakes lie entwined, people who want to get rid of their dirt are assembling. This pond, hence, resembles the form of Siva Sakti. Entering this, our bangles and anklets jingling, our bodies horripilating, let us bathe creating rising waves in the waters!

राग : शुद्धधन्यासी Rāga : Suddhadhanyāsi

14. कादार्कुऴै आड, पैंपूण् कलन् आड,
कोदै कुऴल् आड, वण्डिन् कुऴा आड,
शीतप्पुनल् आडि, शिट्रंबलं पाडि
वेदप्पोरुळ् पाडि, अप्पोरुळ् आमा पाडि
शोदित्तिऱं पाडि, शूऴ् कोन्नै त्तार्पाडि
आदित्तिऱंपाडि, अन्तं आमा पाडि
पेदित्तुनंमै वळर्त्तु येडुत्त पेय् वळै-तन्
पादत्तिऱंपाडि आडु - येल् ओर् येंपावाय्

Kādārkuḷai āḍa, paimpūṇ kalan āḍa
Kódai kuzhal āda vaṇḍin kuzhām āḍa
Śītappunal āḍi śiṭṛambalam pādi
Védapporuḷ pāḍi, apporuḷ āmā pāḍi
Śodittiram pāḍi, śūzh koṇvaittārpāḍi
Ādittaiṛam pāḍi antam āmā pāḍi
Pédittu nammai vaḷarttu yeḍutta peyvaḷai-tan
Pādattiṛampāḍi, āḍu - yel or yempāvāi

14. Kaataar Kuzhaiyaada

Let us bathe in these cold waters, our earrings and other ornaments swinging and our hair and the swarm of bees that sought it dancing.

Thereafter, let us sing of the Lord of Chidambaram, the crux of Vedas, the Embodiment of radiance, the crescent crested One, who is the beginning and the end, so as to make us deserving of His love and grace!

Let us also sing of the lotus feet of the Divine Mother, who separates us from Maya, the cosmic illusion and protects us.

राग : हुसेनी

Rāga : Huséni

15. ओरो रुकाल् "येंपेरुमान्" येन्रु येन्रे, नंपेरुमान्
शीर् ओरु काल्वाय् ओवाळ्, चित्तं कळि कूर,
नीर् ओरु काल् ओवा नेडुं तारै कण् पनिप्प,
पार् ओरु काल् वन्दनैयाळ्, विण्णोरैत्तान् पणियाळ्!
पेर् अरैयर्क्कु इङ्ङने पित्तु ओरुवर आंआरुम्
आर् ओरुवर्? इव्वण्णं आट्कोळ्ळुं वित्तकर्ताळ्,
वार् उरुवप्पूण् मुलैयीर्, वाय् आर नां पाडि,
येर् उरुवप्पूंपुनल् पाय्न्दु आडु - येल ओर् येंपावाय्

Ororukāl "yemperumān" yenṛu yenré, namperumān
Śīr óru kālvāi óvāl chittam kaḷi kūra,
Nīr orukāl ovā nedum tārai kaṇ panippa,
Pār oru kāl vandanaiyāl viṇṇóraittān paṇiyāl
Pér araiyarkku ingane pittu oruvar ām āṛum
Ār oruvar? ivvaṇṇam ātkoḷḷum vittakartāl
Vār uruvappūṇ mulaiyīr, vāi ār nām pāḍi
Yér uruvappunal pāindu ādu - yél ór yempāvāi!

15. Ororukaal

This girl sometimes incessantly chants the name of Lord Siva saying "He is my Lord! He is my Lord!" At other times she recites His glories, yet another time she sits shedding tears due to ecstatic bliss, at other times she lies on the ground unconscious. She does not care for anyone but Lord Siva, however big He may be. She is obsessed with Him.

O! Girls with covered breasts! Let us bathe in the waters filled with flowers singing the praises of the holy feet of the Lord, the Embodiment of knowledge and wisdom, who captivates one and all.

राग : अमृतवर्षिणी Rāga : Amritavarshini

16. मुन्निकडलै, शुरुक्कि येल़ुन्दु, उडैयाळ्

येन्नत्तिगल़्न्दु, येंमै आळुडैयान् इट्टिडैयिन्

मिन्निप्पोलिन्दु, येंपिराट्टि तिरुवडिमेल्

पोन् अं शिलंबिल् शिलंबि, तिरुप्पुरुवम्

येन्नच्चिलैकुलवि, नं तंमै आळ् उडैयाळ्

तन्निल् पिरिवु इला यें कोमान् अन्बर्क्कु

मुन्नि, अवळ् नमक्कु मुन् शुरक्कुं इन् अरुळे

यैन्नप्पोलि़याय् मल़ै - येल् ओर् येंपावाय्!

Munnikkaḍalai, śurukki yezhundu, uḍaiyāḷ

Yennattigazhndu, yemmai āḷudaiyān iṭṭidaiyin

Minnip polindu, yempirāṭṭi ṭiruvaḍi mél

Pon am śilambil śilambi tiruppuruvam

Yennachchilaikulavi, nam tammai āḷ uḍaiyāḷ

Tannil pirivu itā yem komān anbarkku

Munni, avaḷ namakku mun śurakkum in aruḷé

Yenneppozhiyāi mazhai - yél or yempāvāi

16. Munnikkadalai

O! Cloud! Draining the oceans of water you ascend and shine like the black body of Mother Uma! Your lightning is like Her slender waist, you thunder like the jingling of Her anklets. Your rainbow is like Her beautiful brows! You rain showers like the grace of the Mother and Her everunited Spouse Siva!

राग : वसन्त भैरवी

Rāga : Vasanta Bhairavi

17. शेंकणवन्पाल, दिशैमुखन् पाल
येङ्गुं इलादतु ओर् इन्बं नंपालता
कोङ्गु उन् करुङ्कुल्लि! नं तम्मैक्कोताट्टि
इङ्गु नं इल्लङ्गळ् तीरुं येल़ुन्दरुळि,
शें कमलप्पोन्पादं तन्दरुळुं शेवकनै,
अं कण् अरशै, अडियोङ्गट्कु आर् अमुदै,
नङ्गळ् पेरुमानै, पाडि, नलं तिगल़्,
पङ्गयप्पूंपुनल् पाय्न्दु आडु - येल् ओर् येंपावाय्

Śém kaṇavanpāl, diśaimukhan pāl
Yengum itādatu ór inbam nampālatā
Kongu un kavunkuḷali nam tammaikkótaṭṭi
Ingu nam illangal tórum yezhundaruḷi,
Śem kamalapponpādam kandurulum śévakanai
Amkaṇ araśai, aḍiyonkatku ār amudai,
Nangaḷ perumānai, pāḍi nalam tigazha
Pangayappūm punal pāindu ādu - yél or yempāvāi

17. Senkanavanpaal

O! Girl with the fragrant black hair! Lord Siva has bestowed us bliss which we cannot get elsewhere: even from Vishnu, Brahma and other angels.

Being indulgent to us, He has visited our homes and given us the opportunity to worship His lotuslike feet.

Let us sing of that Lord, that Master with the beautiful eyes, who is like nectar to us, His devotees, Our Leader, to spread auspicious prosperity everywhere and bathe in this pond filled with lotuses.

राग : साम | Rāga : Sāma

18. अण्णामलैयान् अडिक्कमलं शेन्रु इरैञ्चुम्
विण्णोर्मुडियिन् मणित्तोकै वीरुअट्राल् पोल्
कण् आर् इरवि कतिर् वन्दु कार् करप्प,
तण् आर् ओळि मयङ्गि, तारकैकळ्-तां अगल
पेण आगि, आण् आय्, अलि आय्, पिरङ्गु, ओळि शेर्
विण् आगि, मण् आगि इत्तनैयुं वेरु आगि,
कण् आर् अमुदमुं आय् निन्रान् कऴल् पाडि,
पेण्णे! इप्पूंपुनल् पाय्न्दु आडु - येल् ओर् येंपावाय्

Aṇṇāmalaiyān aḍikkamalam śenṛu iṛainchum
Viṇṇor mudiyin maṇiṭṭokai vīṛu aṭṛāl pol
Kan ār iravi katir vandu kār karappa,
Taṇ ār oḷi mayangi, tārakaikal-tām agala
Pen āgi, āṇ āi, ali āi piṛangu oḷi śér
Viṇ āgi, maṇāgi ittanaium, véruāgi
Kaṇ ār amudamum āi, ninṛān kazhal pāḍi,
Peṇṇé! ippūmpunal pāindu ādu - yél ór yempāvāi!

18. Annamalaiyaan

O! Girl! The gems on the jewelled crowns of the angels prostrating before the lotus feet of the Lord who resides in Tiruvannamalai become dim amd lustreless.

When the sun comes out with his rays, mist and fog disappear, the stars fade away.

Hence let us sing of the holy feet of our Lord, who though manifests as woman, man, hermaphrodite, heaven, earth etc and yet is beyond all this and is nectar to our eyes, and bathe in these new waters!

राग : वसन्त Rāga : Vasanta

19. "उन् कैयिर् पिळ्ळै उनक्के अडैक्कलं" येन्रु
अङ्गु अप्पलं शोल पुदुक्कुं यें अच्चत्ताल्
येङ्गळ् पेरुमान् उनक्कु ओन्रु उरैप्पों, केळ्!
यें कोङ्गैनिन् अन्बर् अल्लार्तोळ् शेरर्क;
यें कै उनक्कु अल्लातु योप्पणियुं शेय्यर्क
कङ्गुल्, पगल् येंकण् मट्रुं ओन्रुं काणर्क
इङ्गु इप्परिशे येमक्कु येंकोन् नल्कुतियेल्
येङ्गु येल्लिल् येन् ज्ञायिरु येमक्कु? - येल् ओर् येंपावाय्

Un kaiyir pillai unakke adaikkalam yenṛu
Angu appaḻam śol pudukkum yem achchattāl
Yengal perumān unakku onṛu uraippom, keḷ!
Yem kongainin anbar allār toḷ śéraṛka;
Yem kai unakku allādu yeppaṇiyum śeyyaṛka
Kangul, pagal yem kaṇ maṭṛum onṛum kāṇaṛka
Ingu ippariśe yemakku yemkon nalkutiyel
Yengu yezhil yen jnayiṛu yemakku? - yél or yempāvāi

19. Ungaiyirpillai

O! Lord! We hesitate to say that you are ours, just as it is not apt to say to a mother that her child belongs to her. Yet we wish to say one thing. Please listen to it. No one other than you can be our husband. Our hands cannot serve anyone but you. Day and night, we should not see anything but your vision. If you grant us this boon, we wouldn't bother wherever the sun rises!

राग : मध्यमावती — Rāga : Madhyamāvati

20. पोट्रि! अरुळुक निन् आदि आं पाद मलर्
पोट्रि! अरुळुक निन् अन्तं आं शेंतळिर्गळ्
पोट्रि! येल्ला उयिर्क्कुं तोट्रं आं पोन् पादम्
पोट्रि! येल्ला उयिकर्कुं बोगं आं पूं कऴ्ल्कळ्
पोट्रि! येल्ला उयिर्क्कुं इऱु आं इणै-अडिकळ्
पोट्रि! माल्, नान् मुखनुं काणात पुण्डरीकम्
पोट्रि! यां उय्य, आट्कोण्डरुळुं पोन्मलर्कळ्
पोट्रि! यां मार्कऴि नीर् आडु - येल् ओर् येंपावाय्

Poṭṛi! aruḷuka nin ādi ām pāda malar
Poṭṛi! aruḷuka nin antam ām śentaḷirgal
Poṭṛi! yellā uyirkkum toṭṛam ām pon pādam
Poṭṛi! yellā uyirkkum logam am pūm kazhalkaḷ
Poṭṛi! yellā uyirkkum iṛu ām iṇai aḍikaḷ
Poṭṛi! māl nānmukhanum kāṇāta puṇḍarīkam
Poṭṛi! yām uyya, atkondarulum pon malarkal
Poṭṛi! yām mārkazhi nīr ādu - yél or yempāvāi

20. Potri aruluka

Salutations to Your lotus feet, which are the beginning of everything! Let them bless us with grace!

Salutations to your tender red lotus feet, which are the end of everything! Let them bless us with grace!

Salutations to your golden feet, which are the cause of manifestation of all beings!

Salutations to your lotus feet, which protect all beings!

Salutations to your holy feet, which are the end of all beings!

Salutations to your lotus feet, which could not be seen by Vishnu and Brahma!

Salutations to your golden lotus feet, which rule us and bless us.

Salutations to You, who blessed us to bathe in this month of *Margasirsa.**

*December 15 to January 15.

राग : भूपालं Rāga: Bhoopālam

21. पोट्रि ! येन् वाऴ् मुदल् आगिय पोरुळे !

पुलर्न्ददु; पूङ्कऴर् किणै तुणै मलर्कोण्डु

येट्रि निन् तिरुमुखत्तेमक्करुळ् मलरुम्

येऴिल् नगै कोण्डुनिन् तिरुवडि तोऴुकोम्;

शेट्रिदऴ्क्कमलंकण् मलरुंतण् वयल् शुऴ्

तिरुप्पेरुन्तुरैयुरै शिवपेरुमाने !

येट्रुयर्कोडियुडैयाय् ! येमै उडैयाय् !

येंपेरुमान् ! पळ्ळि येऴुन्दरुळाये !

Poṭṛi! yén vāzhmudal āgiya porule!

Pularṇdadu pūnkazhaṛ kiṇai tuṇai malarkoṇdu

Yeṭri nin tirumukhattemakkaruḷ malarum

Yezhil nagai konḍu nin tiruvaḍi tozhukom;

Śetridazhkkamalankaṇ malarum taṇ vayal śūzh

Tirupperunturaiyuṛai śivaperumāne!

Yéṭṛuyar koḍiyuḍaiyāi! yemai uḍaiyāi!

Yemperumān! paḷḷi yezhundaruḷāye!

21. Potri yen

Salutations! O! Lord who is the root cause of my existence!

The dawn has broken. Offering the apt fragrant flowers at your lotus feet and seeing the auspicious smile on your face, we bow before you.

O! Lord Siva! who reside in the temple of Tirupperundurai, full of fields surrounded by lotuses blossoming in dirt!

O! Master! who have the bull on your flag!

O! Leader who rule our lives! Please wake up from your sleep and bless us.

राग : केदारं | Rāga : Kedāram

22. अरुणन् इन्दिरन् दिशै अणुगिनन्; इरुळ पोय्
अगन्रतु; उदयं निन्मलर्त्तिरू मुखत्तिन्
करूणैयिन् सूरियन् येऴ् येऴ् नयनक्
कटिमलर, मट्रण्णल् अङ्कण्णाम्
तिरळ् निरै अरूपद मुरल्वन; इवैयोर्
तिरुप्पेरुन्तुरैयुरै शिवपेरुमाने;
अरूळ् निधि तरवरूं आनन्द मलैये;
अलैकडले; पळ्ळि येऴुन्दरुळाये!

Aruṇan indiran diśai aṇuginan; iruḷ poy
Aganṛatu; udayam nin malarttiru mukhattin
Karaṇaiyin sūriyan yezhayezha, nayanak
Kaṭimalara, maṭraṇṇal ankaṇṇam
Tiraḷ nirai aṛupadam muralvana; ivaiyór
Tirupperunturaiyuṛai śivaperumané;
Aruḷ nidhi taravarum ānanda malaiye;
Alai kaḍalé; paḷḷi yezhundaruḷāyé!

22. Arunan Indiran

The sun has risen in the east, like the compassion in your face! Darkness has disappeared.

The lotuses which have opened like your holy eyes are besieged by bees!

O! Lord of Tirupperundurai! who bestow us the treasure of your grace and appear as the mountain of bliss! O! Ocean of mercy! Wake up from your sleep and bless us!

राग : बिलहरि Rāga : Bilahari

23. कूविन पूङ्कुयिल्; कूविन कोऴि
कुरुकुकल् इयंपिन; इयंपिन शङ्खम्;
ओविन तारकै ओळि; ओळि उदयत्तु
ओरुप्पडुकिन्रतु; विरुप्पोडु नमक्कुत्
देव! नर्चेरिकऴट्राळिणै काट्टाय्;
तिरुप्पेरुन्तुरैयुरै शिवपेरुमाने!
यावरुं अरिवरियाय्; येमक्केळियाय्;
येंपेरुमान्; पळ्ळियेऴुन्दरुळाये!

Kūvina pūnkuyil; kūvina kozhi;
Kurukukaḷ iyampina iyampina sankham
Ovina tārakai oḷi; oḷi udayattu
Orupppadukinṛatu; viruppoḍu namakkut
Deva! narcerikazhaṭrāḷiṇai kāṭṭāi;
Tirupperunturaiyuṛai śivaperumane!
Yāvarum aṛivaṛiyai; yemakkeḷiyāi;
Yemperumān; paḷḷiyezhundaruḷāyé!

23. Koovina poonguyil

The koels and the cocks are crowing. The birds are chirping. The conches are sounding. Due to the spread of the sun's rays, the stars have lost their lustre.

O! Lord of Tirupperundurai! Who is not easily discernible by all others, but accessible to us!

Wake up from your sleep and bless us, showing your pair of feet wearing the strong anklets!

राग : देवगान्धांरी

Rāga : Devagāndhāri

24. इन्निशै वीणैयर् यालि्नर् ओरुपाल्;
इरुक्कोडु तोत्तिरं इयंपिनर. ओरुपाल्;
तुन्निय पिणैमलक्कैयिनर् ओरुपाल;
तो ल्ु कैयर् अल्ु कैयर् तुवळ्कैयर् ओरुपाल्;
चेन्नियिल् अञ्जलि कूप्पिनर् ओरुपाल्
तिरुप्पेरुन्तुरैयुरै शिवपेरुमाने!
येन्नैयुं आण्डुकोण्डु इन्नरुळ् पुरियुम्
येंपेरुमान्; पळि्ळ येल्ुन्दरुळाये!

Inniśai vīṇaiyar yazhinar orupāl;
Irukkoḍu tottiram iyampinar orupāl;
Tunniya piṇaimalarkkaiyinar orupāl;
Tozhukaiyar azhukaiyar tuvaḷkaiyar orupāl;
Chenniyil anjali kūppinar orupāl
Tirupperunturaiyuṛai śivaperumāne!
Yennaiyum āṇḍukoṇḍu innaruḷ puriyum
Yemperumān; paḷḷiyezhundaruḷāyé!

24. Innisai

Some are playing on the veena, some on the flute and other instruments.

Some are reciting the Vedas.

Some are waiting with garlands of flowers.

Some are bowing in blissful devotion.

Yet others are crying in ecstasy.

Due to excessive devotion, some hands in the act of bowing are falling off.

O! Lord of Tirupperundurai! Please wake up from your sleep to bless all these persons, as also to rule over me.

राग : यदुकुलकाम्बोधि Rāga : Yadukulakāmbodhi

25. भूतङ्गळ् तोरुं निन्राय् येनिन् अल्लाल्
"पोक्किलन् वरविलन्" येन निनै प्पुलवोर्
गीतङ्गळ् पाडुतल् आडुतल् अल्लाल्
केट्टरियों उनैक्कण्डरि वारैच्
चीतङ्कोळ् वयल् तिरुप्पेरुन्तुरै मन्नार्
शिन्तनैक्कुं अरियाय्! येङ्कण्मुन् वन्तु
येतङ्कळ् अरुत्तेंमै आण्डरुळ् पुरियुम्
येंपेरुमान्; पळ्ळि येलुन्दरुळाये!

Bhūtangaḷ toruninṛāi yenin allāl
"Pokkilan varavilan" yena ninaippulavor
Gītangaḷ pādutal ādutal allāl
Keṭṭaṛiyóm unaikkaṇḍaṛivāraic
Chītankol vayal tirupperunturai mannār
Śintanaikkum ariyāi! yenkaṇmun vantu
Yétankaḷ aṛuttemmai āṇḍaruḷ puriyum
Yemperumān; paḻḻi yezhundaruḷāyé!

25. Bhootangal thorum

You are present in the five elemental powers! You are the One with no income and expenditure! so say in praise the learned ones!

When devotion grows, some sing, some dance! But we have not heard of anyone who has seen you face to face.

O! Lord of Tirupperundurai, surrounded by cool green fields! You, who are so difficult even to imagine! Please wake up from your sleep and come and bless us so that we can see you.

राग : खमाज़ Rāga : Khamās

26. पप्पऱ् वीट्टिरुन्दुणरुं निन् अडियार्
पन्दनै वन्दऱुत्तार् अवर् पलरुम्
मैप्पुऱु कण्णियर् मानुडत्तियल्बिन्
वणङ्गुकिन्ऱार्, अणङ्गिन् मणवाळा!
चेप्पुऱु कमलङ्गळ् मलरुन्तण् वयल्शूऴ्,
तिरुप्पेऱुन्तुऱैयुरै शिवपेरुमाने!
इप्पिरप्परुत्तेंमै आण्डरुळ् पुरियुम्
येंपेरुमान् पळ्ळि येऴुन्दरुळाये!

Pappaṛa vīṭṭirundunarum nin aḍiyār
Pandanai vandaṛuttār avar palarum
Maippuṛu kaṇṇiyar mānuḍattiyalbin
Vaṇagukinrār aṇangin maṇavālā!
Cheppuṛu kamalangaḷ malaruntaṇ vayal śūzh
Tirupperunturaiyurai śivaperumāne!
Ippiṛappaṛuttamai āṇḍarul puriyum
Yemperumān paḷḷi yezhuntaruḷāye!

26. Papparaveettirunthu

Your devotees, whose minds have lost their turbulence and are fixed on you, bow before you.

Among them are women who have lost their attachments.

They also feel blissful, bowing before you O! Lord of Uma! O! Lord Siva! Who reside in the temple of Tirupperundurai, which is surrounded by green fields filled with cool waters! Please wake up from your sleep and bless us, tearing asunder our birthborn burden of sorrow.

राग : रीतिगौल Rāga : Rītigowla

27. अतुपऴ्च्चुवैयेन अमुदेन अऱितर्कु
अरिदेन येळिदेन अमररुं अरियार्
ईतु अवन् तिरुवुरु इवन् अवन् येनवे
येङ्गळै आण्डुकोण्डु इङ्गेऴुन्तरुळुम्
मधु वळर पोऴिल् शूऴ् तिरु उत्तर कोश
मङ्गैयुळ्ळाय्! तिरुप्पेरुन्तुरै मन्ना
येतु येमैप्पणि कोळुं आऱतु केट्पोम्;
येंपेरुमान् पळ्ळि येऴुन्तरुळाये!

Atupazhaccuvaiyena amudena aṛitaṛku
Ariden yeḷidena amararum ariyār
Itu avan tiruvuru ivan avan yenave
Yengaḷai āṇḍukoṇḍu ingezhundaruḷum
Madhuvaḷar pozhil śūzh tiru uttara kosa
Mangaiyuḷḷāi! Tirupperunturai mannā
Yetu yemaippaṇi koḷum āṛatu keṭpom;
Yemperumān paḷḷi yezhuntarulāye!

27. Athu pazhacchuvai

"The taste of the Supreme Being is like fruit, He is like nectar, He is hard to know, but easily accessible to His devotees, This is His Divine Form, This is He" so say the angels and still do not know the truth.

But you have appeared here before us out of your kind indulgence to bless us.

O! Lord of Tirupperundurai! Who reside in the temple of Uttarakosamangai! How can we become deserving of your grace? We shall act accordingly.

My Master! Please wake up from your sleep and bless us!

राग : धन्यासी   Rāga : Dhanyāsi

28. मुन्दिय मुदल्नडु इरुदियुं आनाय्
     मूवरुं अरिंकिलर् यावर् मट्ररिंवार् ?
     पन्दणै विरलियुं नीयुं निन्नडियार्
     पऴंकुडिल् तोरुं येऴु ्न्दरु ळिय परने !
     शेन्तऴ्ल् पुरैतिरु मेनियुं काट्टित्
     तिरुप्पेरुन्तुरैयुरै कोयिलुं काट्टि
     अन्तणनावतुं काट्टि वन्ताण्डाय्
     आरमुदे ! पळ्ळियेऴु ्न्तरु ळाये !

Mundiya mudalnadu iṛudiyum ānāi
Mūvarum aṛikilar yāvar maṭṛaṛivār?
Pandaṇai viraliyum nīyum ninnaḍiyār
Pazhamkuḍil toṛum yezhundaruḷiya parane!
Śentazhal puraitiru méniyum kāṭṭit
Tirupperuntuṛaiyuṛai koilum kaṭṭi
Antaṇanāvatum kāṭṭi vantāṇḍāi
Āramude! paḷḷiyezhuntaruḷāye!

28. Muthiyamuthal

O! God! You are the beginning, the middle and the end! When even the Trinity of gods cannot know you, how can anyone know you?

Such a rare Being like you come into each of the poor huts of your devotees, accompanied by Uma, the embodiment of grace, in order to bless your devotees.

O! Lord! who has captivated us with your crimson fiery form and the holy temple of Tirupperundurai! Please wake up from your sleep and bless us.

राग : सौराष्ट्र

Rāga : Saurāshtra

29. विण्णकत्तेवरुं नण्णवुं माट्टा
विऴुप्पोरुळे! उन तोऴुप्पडि योङ्गळ
मण्णकत्तेवन्दु वाऴ्च्चेय्ताने!
वण्तिरुप्पेरुन्तुरैयाय्! वऴियडियों
कण्णकत्तेनिन्नु कळितरुतेने!
कडलमुदे करुं पेविरुंपडियार्
येण्णगत्ताय्! उलगुक्कुयिरानाय्!
येंपेरुमान् पळ्ळि येऴुन्दरुळाये!

Viṇṇakattévarum naṇṇavum māṭṭā
Vizhupporuḷé! un tozhuppaḍi yóngaḷ
Maṇṇakatté vandu vāzhachcheitāne!
Vaṇtirupperunturaiyāi! Vazhiyaḍiyom
Kaṇṇakatteninṛu kaḷitaruténé!
Kaḍalamudé! karum pevirum paḍiyar
Yeṇṇagattāi! ulagukkuyirānāi!
Yemperumān paḷḷi yezhuntarulāye!

29. Vinnagathe varum

O! Supreme Being! Who cannot be approached even by the angels in heaven!

You who caused us to be born in this earth!

O! Lord who resides in Tirupperundurai!

You who are like honey to the thirsty eyes of your devotees for generations which we are.

O! Lord who are like the ambrosia, risen from the milky ocean!

You who reside in the hearts of your devotees who yearn for you!

O! Lord who are the life of all the worlds!

Please wake up from your sleep and bless us.

राग : मध्यमावती Rāga : Madhyamāvati

30. भुवनियिर्पोय् पिऱवामैयिन् नाळ् नाम्
पोक्कुकिन्रों अवमे इन्द भूमि
शिवनुय्यक्कोळ्किन्र वाऱेन्रु नोक्कि
तिरुप्पेरुन्तुऱैयुऱै वाय्तिरुमालाम्
अवन् विरुप्पेय्दवुं मलरवन् आशै
पडवुं निन्नलर्न्द मेय्क्करुणैयुं नीयुम्
अवनियिर्पुकुन्देमै आट्कोळ्ळ वल्लाय्!
आरमुदे पळ्ळि येऴुन्दरुळाये!

Bhuvaniyiṛpói piravāmaiyin nāḷnām
Pokkukinrom avame inda bhūmi
Śivanuyyakkoḷkinra vāṛenṛu nókki
Tirupperunturaiyuṛai vāitirumālām
Avam viruppeidavum malaravan āśai
Paḍavum ninnalarnda meikkaruṇaiyum nīyum
Avaniyirpukundemai ātkoḷla vallāi!
Āramude paḷḷiyezhundaruḷāyé!

30. Bhuvaniyir

O! Immortal One! This earth has been given to us by Lord Siva so that we can ascend to liberation.

Vishnu and Brahma are regretting that they are spending their days in vain without being born in this earth.

O! Lord who resides in Tirupperundurai! You who, out of your deep and extensive compassion, have come to this earth in order to rule us.

Please wake up from your sleep and bless us!

SONGS OF JNANESHWAR

(13th Century A.D.)

	Song	*Rāga*
1.	Om Namoji aadyaa	Lalita
2.	Soniyacha divas aajee	Suddhakalyan
3.	Avaghaachi saunsaar	Bhimpalas
4.	Roop paahtaa lochani	Yamankalyan
5.	Samacharan sundar	Bagesree
6.	Ek tattva naam	Sankara
7.	Baravaa ho hari	Bhimpalas
8.	Konaache he roop	Marubihag
9.	Parvataa pramaane	Abhogi
10.	Aataa Visvaatmake deve	Bhairavi

JNANESWAR

JNANESHWAR (1275-1296 A.D.)

Jnaneshwar was the famous mystic philosopher-poet-saint of Maharashtra, who, despite a short life of 22 years, has bequeathed a legacy of immortal works that remains an inspiration to the people of Maharashtra to this day.

His three important works are: *Jnāneshwari*, a monumental yet simple commentary on the Bhagavat Gita, *Anubhavamrita,* in which he explains his philosophy of life and *Abhangs* or devotional lyrics.

Jnaneshwar may be considered the philosophic founder of the Bhakti movement in Maharashtra, of which other luminaries are: Namdev (a contemporary of Jnaneshwar), Eknath and Tukaram. Jnaneshwar's ideal of Bhakti is unique. It is not merely a subjective feeling, but the heart of reality, the *summum bonum* of life. Bhakti or God-devotion or God-intoxication is the root of all moral qualities.

Jnaneshwar saw no conflict between Bhakti and the concept of Advaita.

The universe is, according to Jnaneshwar, an expression of God's love for Himself.

As water sports with itself in the form of waves, the *ātman* or the Universal Soul plays with itself in the form of the universe and feels happy. God has become man to experience His own affection. One need not forsake the world to find God.

Human life is a precious gift of God. It should be kept pure and holy. The summit of all virtues is God-devotion. There is no object of love greater than God.

In the pathway of loving devotion, the organs of the senses and the tempers of the mind are turned towards God and become vehicles of His love.

According to Jnaneshwar, the God-intoxicated become like moons without spots and suns without the scorching heat. Jnaneshwar's religion of love is a unique contribution to mankind.

राग : ललित Rāga : Lalita

1. ओम् नमोजी आद्या। वेदप्रतिपाद्या।।

जय जय स्वसंवेद्या। आत्मरूपा।।

देवा तूचि गणेशू। सकलमतिप्रकाशू।।

म्हणोनि निवृत्तिदासू। अवधारिजोजी।।

अकार चरण युगल। उकार उदर विशाल।।

मकार महामंडल। मस्तकाकारे।।

हे तिन्ही एकवटले। तेथ शब्दब्रह्म कवळ्ले।।

ते मियां श्रीगुरुकृपा नमिले। आदिबीज।।

Om namoji ādyā/ veda pratipādyā//
Jaya Jaya Swasamvedyā/ ātmarupa//
Devā tūchi gaṇéshū/ sakalamatiprakāshu//
Mhaṇoni nivrittidāsū/ avadharijojī//
Akār charaṇ yugaḷ/ ukār udar viśal//
Makār mahāmaṇdal/ mastakākāré//
Hé tinhī ékavatalé/ teth shabdabrahma kavalale//
Té miya Śrīgurukripā namiḷe/ ādibeej//

1. Om Namojee aadyaa

Prostrations to the Primordial Eternal One, discussed by the Vedas! Victory to You O! Lord who are self-born and reside in me and all living beings!

You are Lord Ganesa! who shine as the beacon of knowledge! Accept my humble prayer and grant beatitude!

Your feet form the letter A, your large stomach the letter U and your shining crest is the letter M.

The combination of the three: AUM, the Pranava Sound is the holy beginning of the universe!

With blessings from my Auspicious Guru, I bow before this primordial seed of the universe!

राग : शुद्धकल्याण Rāga: Suddhakalyān

2. सोनियाचा दिवस आजी। अमृते पाहिला॥

नाम आठविता रुपे, प्रगत पै झाला।

गोपाला रे तुझे ध्यान, ध्यान लागो मना॥

अणु न विसंबे हरी, जगत्रय जीवना।

गोपाला रे तुझे ध्यान, ध्यान लागो मना॥

तनु मनु शरण तुझ्या विनटलो पायी।

बापरखुमादेवीवरावाचुनि अणु नेने कांही।

गोपाला रे तुझे ध्यान, ध्यान लागो मना॥

Soniyāchā divas ājī amruté pāhila
Nām āthavitā rupe, pragat pai jhālā
Gópāla ré tujhé dhyāṇ, dhyān lāgo manā
Aṇu na visambe harī, jagatraya jivanā
Gopāla ré tujhe dhyān dhyān lāgó manā
Tanu manu śaraṇ tujhyā vinatalo pāyī
Bāparakhumādevī varā vāchūni aṇu néné kānhī
Gopāla ré tujhé dhyān dhyān lāgo manā

2. Soniyacha divas aajee

This is the golden day when I got the nectar of bliss! As I was thinking of the Lord and chanting His name, He came and stood before me!

O! Lord Gopala! let your form ever remain in my mind, as I pray and meditate!

O! Hari! without wasting a second, you look after the welfare of all beings in the three worlds!

O! Gopala! let your form ever remain in my mind, as I pray and meditate!

With my body and soul, I surrender at your feet!

Other than my father Vitthala, the Lord of Rakhuma Devi, I do not think of anything else.

O! Lord Gopala! let your form ever remain in my mind, as I pray and meditate!

राग : भीमपलास Rāga : Bhimpalās

3. अवघाचि संसार। सुखाचा करीन
आनन्दे भरीन। तिन्ही लोक॥ धृ॥
जाईन गे माये, तया पंढरपुरा
भेटेन माहेरा। आपुलिया॥ १॥
सर्व सुकृताचे। फल मी लाहीन।
क्षेम मी देईन। पांडुरंगी।। २॥
बापररवुमादेवीवर-विट्ठलाचे भेटी
आपुलिया संवसाटी। येउनि राहीन॥

Avaghāchi saunsār Sukhacha kareen
Ānande bharin Tinhī lok
Jāyīn gé māyé, tayā Pandharpurā
Bhéten mahérā āpuliyā
Sarva sukrutāche phal mee lāhin
Kshem mi deein Pāṇḍurangī
Bāparakhumādévivar Viththalāche bheti
Apuḷiyā Samvasāti yeouni raahin

3. Avaghaachi saunsaar

I shall try to make this world a happy one!

I shall fill with happiness all the three worlds!

I shall go to Pandharpur to see Lord Vitthala!

There I shall meet all my family members!

I shall enjoy the fruits of all good deeds done and I shall give the credit fot this to Lord Panduranga!

To see my father Lord Vitthala, Lord of Rakhumadevi and be near Him, I shall stay in Pandharpur. This is for my good.

राग : यमनकल्याण Rāga : Yamankalyān

4. रूप पाहता लोचनी। सुख झाले वो साजणी॥
तो हा विठ्ठल बरवा। तो हा माधव बरवा।।
बहुत सुकृताची जोडी। म्हणुनी विठ्ठली आवडी।।
सर्व सुखाचे आगर। बापरखुमादेवीवर॥

Rūp pāhtā lochanī sukh jhale vó saajaṇī/
To hā viththal baravā tó hā mādhav baravā//
Bahut sukritācī joḍī mhaṇunī viththalī avāḍī/
Sarva sukhāche āgar bāpa rakhumā dévīvar//

4. Roop paahtaa lochani

Seeing the Lord's form with my eyes, I am filled with immense joy!

He is the good, kind Vitthal! He is the good and kind Madhava, the Lord of Lakshmi!

To be good and do good is what pleases Vitthal!

He, my Father and the Lord of Rakhumadevi, is the garden of joy. To be with Him is bliss!

राग : वागेश्री Rāga : Vāgésri

5. समचरण सुन्दर। कासे ल्याला पितांबर।
अनादिया माळा रुळती। मुख्य त्यात वैजयंती॥
मुख मंडलाची शोभा। कोटिसूर्य ऐसी प्रभा।
काय मागावे आणिक। उभे ठाके मोक्ष सुख॥
उरी वत्साचे लांछन। ऐसा उभा नारायण।
हाती धरीतो आयुधा। शंख चक्र पद्म गदा॥
धन्य झाली माझी भवती। वोलंगिल्या चारी मुक्ती।
पसरोनि दोन्ही बाहो। अलिंगिला पंढरीरावो॥

Samacharaṇ sundar kāse lyaalā pitāmbar
Anādiyā mālā ruḷatī mukhya tyat vaijayantī
Mukh maṇḍalāchī śobhā koṭi sūrya aisī prabhā
Kaay māgāvé āṇik ubhé thāke mokshasukh
Urī vatsāché lānchan aisā ubha Nārāyaṇ
Hātī dharīto āyudhā śankha chakra padma gadā
Dhanya jhāḷī mājhī bhakti volangilya chārī muktī
Pasaroni donhī bāho alingiḷa pandhari rāvo

5. Samacharan sundar

Lord Panduranga (who stands on the brick) has beautiful feet. He wears the yellow garment.

Around His neck are many garlands and necklaces, the most prominent being Vaijayanti (Tulsi).

His facial radiance is like the light of a million suns!

What more can I ask, when the eternal joy of salvation is before me?

He has the Vatsa (stain) mark on His chest! Lord Narayana stands before me!

He holds the conch, disc, the lotus and the mace in His hands!

My devotion has been blessed by the Lord!

The four gateways to liberation have cleared the path for me to be with Him!

With open arms, I am able to embrace the Lord of Pandhari!

राग : शंकर Rāga : Sankara

6. एक तत्त्व नाम दृढ धरी मना।
हरीसी करुणा येईल तुझी॥
ते नाम सोपे रे, राम कृष्ण गोविंद।
वाचेसी सदगद, जपे आधी॥
नामापरते तत्त्वनाहीरे अन्यथा।
वाया आणिक पंथा जाशील झणी॥
ते नाम सोपे रे राम कृष्ण गोविंद।
ज्ञानदेव मौन जपमाळ अंतरी॥
धरोनि श्रीहरी जपे सदा।
ते नाम सोपे रे राम कृष्ण गोविन्द॥

Ek Tattva nām drudh dharī manā
Harīsī karuna yeīl tujhi
Té nām sopé ré Rām Krishṇa Govinda
Vāchesi sadgad, jape ādhī
Nāmā parte tattva nahīre anyathā
Vāyā āṇik panthā jāśīl jhaṇi
Te nām sope re Rām Krishṇa Govinda
Jnānadev maun japamāl antarī
Dharóni Śrīharī jape sadā
Te nām sope re Rām Krishṇa Govinda

6. Ek Tattva nam

Let the mind firmly hold one principle of worship: Chant the name of the Lord!

Hari, the Lord will be kind to you!

The name is so easy to chant: Rama, Krishna, Govinda! See that your thoughts and words are pure, before you begin to chant!

Other than chanting the name of the Lord, there is no easy path of worship!

If you forget the Lord, you go astray after vain desires! But chanting the Lord's name is so easy: Rama, Krishna, Govinda!

Jnanadev says: Chant the Lord's name silently in your heart! And let the thoughts focus always on Hari!

The Lord's name is so easy to chant: Rama, Krishna, Govinda!

राग : भीमपलास Rāga : Bhīmpalās

7. बरवा हो हरी बरवा हो। गोविंद गोपाल गुण गरवा हो॥
सावळा हो हरी सावळा हो। मदनमोहन कान्हु गोवळा हो॥
गोविन्द, गोपाल॥
पाहता हो हरी पाहता हो। ध्यान लागलिया चित्ता हो॥
गोविंद, गोपाल॥
पडिले हो हरी पडिले हो। बापरखुमादेवीवर जडिले हो॥
गोविंद, गोपाल॥

Baravā ho harī baravā ho, govind gopāḷ guṇ garavā ho
Sāvaḷā ho harī sāvaḷā ho, madanmohan kānhu govaḷā ho//
Govind, Gopāl
Pāhtā ho harī pāhtā ho, dhyān lāgliyā chitta ho//
Govind, Gopāl
Padiḷe ho harī padiḷe ho, bāp rakhumādevīvar Jadiḷe ho//
Govind, Gopāl

7. Baravaa ho Hari

Hari is so nice! It is a joy to sing of the good qualities of Govinda! Gopala (the Lord)!

When I gaze at Him, my mind rests on Him alone!

He is darkhued! He is handsome and charming!

My mind is enamoured by Him and my heart is at His feet!

He is the Lord of Rakhumadevi and my Father!

It is a joy to sing of the good qualities of the Lord who is Govinda! Gopāla!

राग : मारुविहाग

Rāga : Mārubihāg

8. कोणाचे हे रूप देह हा कोणाचा
आत्माराम त्याचा तोचि जाणे॥
मी तू हा विचार विवेक शोधावा
गोविंदू हा ध्याना, याचि देहि॥
द्येभा ज्ञाना ज्ञान त्रिपुरी वेगळा
सहस्त्रदळी उगवला सूर्य जैसा॥
ज्ञान देवा म्हणे नयनातील ज्योति
भा नमे भूपे ना तुम्ही जाणा॥

Kóṇāche he rūp deh hā koṇāchā
Atmārām tyāchā tochi jāṇe//
Mī tū hā vichār viveke śodhāva
Govindū hā dhyānā yachi dehi//
Dyebhā gnānā gnān tripurī vegḷā
Sahastra daḷi ugwalā sūrya jaisā//
Jnān devā mhaṇe nayanātīḷ jyotī
Bhā name bhūpe nā tumhī jāṇā//

8. Koṇaache he roop

The one who gave the face and form only knows the true nature of this being!

One should use one's discrimination, while considering about you and me!

Try to follow the path shown by Govinda!

A learned person uses his knowledge to better the world. He is like the sun, which shines like a thousand-petalled lotus and illumines the world!

Jnanadeva says: You should know that the light in the eyes (given by the Lord) can help you gain knowledge and help others.

राग : अभोगी

Rāga : Abhogi

९. पर्वताप्रमाणे पातक करणे।
वज्रलेप होणे अभक्तासी
नाहि ज्यासि भक्ति ते पतित अभक्त
हरीसी न भजत दैवहत॥
अनंत वाचाळ बरळती बरळ
त्या कैसा दयाळ पावे हरी॥
ज्ञानदेवा प्रमाण, आत्मा हा निधान
तैसा धरी दृढ, एक नांदे॥

Parvatā pramāṇe pātaka karaṇe/
Vajralep hone abhaktāsī
Nāhi jyāsi bhakti té patit abhakta
Harī sī na bhajat daivahata//
Anant vāchāḷ baraḷatī baraḷ
Tyā kaisa dayāl pāve harī//
Jnānadevā pramāṇ ātmā hā nidhān
Taisā dharī dridh ek nāndé//

9. Parvataa pramaane

Committing mountainous sins is inevitable in the case of hardcore nondevotees of God!

Those whose devotion is not sincere, are as good as nondevotees!

Not worshipping the Lord is their unfortunate lot!

There are many talkative fools who talk nonsense.

How can the kind Lord bless them?

Jnanadeva says: One's own soul is the yardstick to measure the strength of one's devotion!

राग : भैरवी Rāga : Bhairavi

10. आता विश्वात्मके देवे। थेणे वागयज्ञे तोषावे।

तोषोनी मज द्यावे। पसायदान हे॥

जेखळांची व्यकटी सांडो। तया सत्कर्मी रती वाढो।

भूतां परस्परे जडो। मैत्र जीवाचे॥

दुरितांचे तिमिर जावो। विश्व स्वधर्म सूर्ये पाहो।

जो जे वांछील तो ते लाहो। प्राणिजात॥

वर्षत सकलमंगली। ईश्वर निष्ठांची मांदियाळी।

Ātā viswātmake deve/ theṇe vagyajne toshāvé/

Toṣoni maj dyāve/ pasāydān hé//

Jekhaḷanchī vyakaṭī sāndo/ taya satkarmi ratī vāḍho/

Bhūtān paraspare jado/ maitr jīvache//

Duritānche timir jāvo/ viśw swadharm sūrye pāho/

Jó je vānchīḷ to te lāho/ prāṇi jāt//

Varshat sakalamangaḷī/ īśwar nishṭhānchī māndiyāḷī/

10. Aataa Vishvaatmake deve

O! Universal Lord! I hope you are satisfied with my discourse, explaining the Bhagavat Geeta in simple language to the whole world.

If you are really pleased, kindly bless me with the following:

Let the cruel and wicked ones forget their evil thoughts and vices, and turn towards kind deeds and goodness.

Let them be friendly towards all and make friends with everyone!

Let the misfortune of the ill-fated vanish.

Let everyone see the sunlight of duty towards the world!

Let every person's wish be granted!

Let there be a celebration of all devotees!

Let their dedication and devotion to God result in a continuous shower of auspicious things!

अनवरत भूमंण्डळी भेटतु भूता ॥

चला कल्पतरुंचे आरव। चेतना चिंतामणींचे गाव।

बोळते जे अर्णव। पियूषांचे॥

चंद्रमे जे अळांछन। मार्तड जे तापहीन।

ते सर्वांसी सदा सज्जन। सोयरे होतु॥

किंवहुना सर्वसुखी। पूर्ण होऊनी तिन्हीं लोकी।

भजिजो आदिपुरुषी अखंडित॥

अणि ग्रंथोपजीविये विशेषी लोकी इये।

दृष्टादृष्ट विजये हो आवेजी॥

येथ म्हणे श्रीविश्वेश्वरावो। हा होईल दानपसावो।

येणे बरे ज्ञानदेवो। सुखिया झाळा॥

Anavarat bhūmandalī bhétatu bhūta//
Chalā kalpatarunche aarav/ chétna chintamaṇinche gaav/
Bolte je arṇav/ piyūshanché//
Chandrame je alānchhan/ martanḍ jé taapheen/
Te sarvā si sadā sajjan/ soyare hotu//
Kimbahunā sarvsukhī/ Pūrna hoūni tinhī loki/
Bhajijo ādipurushi akhandit//
Aṇi granthopajīviye viśeshī loki iye/
Drishṭādrishṭa vijaye ho āveji//
Yéth mhaṇe śrīviśveśvarāvo/ hā hoīl danpasāvo/
Yene baré Jnandevo/ sukhiyā jhālā//

Let us go to that place where:

there is the forest of wishgranting kalpa trees,

there is the city of Chintamani, where all desires get fulfilled!

the sea is an ocean of nectar (which gives immortality)

Let people be kind and pleasant like the moon and fearless like the sun

Let them always be good and helpful to others!

O! Lord! I pray to you that every soul in the three worlds should be content and ever pray to you!

Perhaps, my mission in this world is complete, I am happy and I thank God for all the good graces and gifts that He has conferred on me!

Let this compendium which is intended for the people be useful to them. If they appreciate it, my work is done!

O! Lord! I ask you to grant me all these and with these humble words, I take your leave.

SONGS OF NARSI MEHTA

(15th Century A.D.)

Song	*Rāga*
1. Vaishnava janato	Khamas
2. Sree Hari Narahari	Hamsadhwani
3. Nahi aapoo ho nandana	Kafi
4. Nirdhan purush	Poorvikalyani
5. Saadhu saache bhajo charan	Malhar
6. Sant Karuna	Tilakkamod
7. Harinaam vinaa	Sohani
8. Jasodaaji jamvaane	Mishra Piloo
9. Samsarano bhay	Jogkauns/Bhimpalas
10. Vaishnav janane vishay bhee	Mishra Khamas

NARSIMEHTA

NARSI MEHTA (1414-1480 A.D.)

Narsi Mehta is the foremost poet-saint of Gujarat.

His songs reveal an intense devotion to Lord Krishna, his chosen Ishtadevata (Favourite Deity).

Narsi Mehta's songs, simple and moving and soaked in the basic philosophy of the Bhakti cult, have become part of the folk tradition of Gujarat.

All his life, Narsi Mehta preached humility, equal compassion for all beings, self-discipline and total devotion to Lord Krishna.

He disregarded caste barriers and social restrictions. He deemed all human beings as children of God, *Harijana.*

He was born at Talaja, a village near Junagadh in Saurashtra, Gujarat. He lost his father at the age of three and his mother at the age of eleven. At the age of fourteen he married a girl named Manekbai. A son and daughter were born to them.

Narsi led a peaceful life in Junagadh, till his wife's death in 1451 A.D. He also lost his children: his son first and his daughter, a few years later.

Narsi Mehta took his bereavements philosophically: "By His grace they have passed away. I feel no sorrow. We all have to leave this mortal frame one day. I can now pursue my devotion to Gopal without interruption", he said.

He danced and sang devotional songs composed by him day and night.

At the age of 53 Narsi left Junagadh and went to live in Mangrol, where he died at the age of 66 years.

The element of Bhakti or devotion, which is primarily a doctrine of adoration of a personalised God (Ishtadevata) which is predominant in Narsi Mehta's songs, is reminiscent of the same emotion in the *pāsurams* of the South Indian Alwars and the *tevarams* of the Nayanars, who lived between 500 A.D. and 900 A.D.*

*Presumably, the Bhakti cult, born in South India, spread first in Karnataka and then to Maharashtra and culminated in Gujarat.

राग : खमाज़

Rāga : Khamās

1. वेष्णव जन तो तेणे कहिये, जे पीड पराई जाणेरे
परदुःखे उपकार करे तोये, मन अभिमान न आणे रे ॥
सकल लोकमां सहुने वंदे, निंदा न करे केनी रे
वाच काछ मन निश्चल राखे, धन धन जननी तेनी रे ॥
समदृष्टि ने तृष्णा त्यागी, परस्त्री जेणे मात रे
जिह्वा थकी असत्य न बोले, परधन नव झाले हाथ रे ॥
मोह माया व्यापे नहीं जेने, दृढ वैराग्य जेना मनमां रे
राम नाम शुं ताळी लागी सकल तीरथ तेना तनमां रे ॥
वण लोभीने कपटरहित छे काम क्रोध निवार्या रे
भणे नरसैयो तेनुं दरसन करता कुल अेकोतर तार्या रे ॥

Vaishṇava jan to teṇe kahiye je peeḍ parāī jāṇé ré
Paraduhkhe upkār kare toye man abhimān na āṇe ré//
Sakal lók mām sahune vande, nindā na kare kénī ré
Vāch kācch man niśchal rākhe dhan dhan jananī tenī ré//
Samadriṣṭi ne triṣṇā tyāgī parastrī jeṇe maat ré
Jihwā thakī asatya na bole par dhan nav jhaale hāth ré//
Moh māyā vyāpe nahīn jene druḍh vairāgya jenā manmā ré
Rām nām shu tāli lāgi sakal tīrath tenā tan mā ré//
Vaṇ lobhīne kapaṭrahit chhe kām krodh nivarya ré
Bhaṇe narasaiyo tenu darsan kartā kul ekoter tārya ré//

1. Vaishnava janato

He is called a man of God, who understands the pain of others.

Having helped another in trouble, does not feel proud of it.

He will be polite to all people and will not condemn or criticise anyone.

He is pure in speech, deed and thought and everyone blesses his mother.

He is equanimous, has given up all desires and looks at women as mothers.

He does not speak untruth and does not covet others' wealth.

Delusion and desire never dominate him, his mind is firm in detachment.

He is ever engaged in chanting God's name and all pilgrim centres are in his body.

He has no greed and no deceit. He has overcome lust and anger.

Narsi says: Seeing such a person sanctifies the entire family lineage.

राग : हंसध्वनि Rāga : Hamsadhwani

2. श्री हरी, नरहरी, कृष्ण कृपा करी
राखो लक्ष्मी वर चरण शरणे
शोक मोहे गया जन्म रुधवा वृथा
दुष्ट चिंता करी उदर भरणे ॥ श्रीहरी
मात तू, तात तू भ्रात तू भूधरा-भगवान
तुज विना अवर कोने न जाणे
दास हूं, नाथ तूं एम समझी सदा
द्वारमां बेसी तुज गुण वखाणि ए॥ श्रीहरी
शरण द्यो श्रीहरी, दीन जाणी करी
सर्वदा दासने चरणे राखो।
बेऊं कर जो डीने नरसैयो विनवे, नित्य,
प्रति नित्य करुणाअे दारवो॥ श्रीहरी

Śrī harī, naraharī, krishṇa kripā karī
Rakho lakshmīvar charan śarane
Śok mohe gayā janm rudhvā vrithā
Dushṭa chintā karī udar bharaṇe// Śrīharī
Māt tū tāt tū, bhrāt tū, bhudharā-bhagawān
Tuj vina avar kone na jāṇe
Dās hoom, nāth tu(m) em samjhī sadā
dwārmān besī tuj guṇ vakhāṇi ye// Śrīharī
Śaraṇ dyó śrīharī dīn jāṇī karī
sarvadā dāsne charne rākho
Beun kar joḍīné narasaiyo vinave, nitya
pratinitya karūṇā ye dārvo// Śrīharī

2. Sree Hari Narahari

O! God! Sree Hari! Narahari! Krishna! Be merciful to me.

O! Lord of Lakshmi! Keep me at your feet!

My life has been wasted in delusion and sorrow,

I was only interested in satisfying my appetite

You are my mother, father and brother!

You are the effulgent Lord who rules the earth

Except you, I do not know anyone else.

I have always understood that I am your servant and you are my Master.

Sitting at the temple door, I sing of your good qualities.

O! God! Sree Hari! Give me refuge! I am poor and helpless.

Keep me always at your feet!

With both hands folded, Narsi beseeches you to bestow your blessing every day!

राग : काफी Rāga : Kāfi

3. नहि आपू हो नंदना लाल। महीडा मारो रे
तू पुटेपुठे मा चाल, अमे नथी तारां रे॥
नारी जीभलडी ना बोल, हैये वागे रे।
नित्य लेवा आवे दाण, शुं मोहन मागे रे।।
अमे रहीजे गोकुलि ये गाम, मथुरा जाई रे।
केम रोके वाट मां चोर? दाण नही दईजे रे।
तू निर्लज्ज चालना लाल, हुं नथी जेवी रे।
कान तारे ने मारे आज, थशे जोवा जेवी रे
वहाले फोडया महीना माट, वस्त्रो ताणी रे
लूटी वनमा सहिदर साथ, राधा राणी रे
जित्या जित्या जुगदाधार, गोपीओ हारी रे
मळ्यो नरसैयोंनो नाथ बटुक ब्रह्मचारी रे

Nahi āpū ho nandanā lāl mahīḍa mārā ré
Tū puṭepuṭhe mā chal, ame nathi tara ré//
Nārī jībhalaḍīna ból haiye vāge ré/
Nitya leva āvé dāṇ śu(n) mohan māge ré//
Ame rahije gokuliye gām mathura jayī ré
Kém roke vāṭ ma chor dāṇ nahī dayīje ré
Tū nirlajj chalna lāl hoo(n) nathī jevī ré
Kān tāre né māre aaj thaśé jenā jévī ré
Vahāle phoḍyā mahīna māt, vastró tāni ré
Lūṭi van mā sahidar sāth rādhā rāṇī ré
Jityā jityā jugadādhār gopīó hārī ré
Malyo narasaiyono nāth baṭuk brahmachāri ré

3. Nahi aapoo ho nandana

(A Gopi from Gokul sings)

I will not give you milk,O! Son of Nanda! O! great Lord!

You may try to be naughty! But we are not of your kind!

Your sweet piercing words have hurt my heart!

Daily you come asking for something. Why are you troubling me?

We keep our cows in Gokul and go to Mathura to sell milk.

Which thief can stop us on the way? Haven't we paid our dues?

You are shameless and mischievous! but I am not like you! Today let us have a quarrel. It will be worth watching!

You break my milkpots by throwing pebbles. You try to pull my saree!

You have troubled Radha when she was with friends in the forest.

You are the saviour of the universe! These Gopis have lost their hearts to you!

But you, the Lord of Narsi, are the child bachelor!

राग : पूर्वीकल्याणी

Rāga : Poorvikalyāni

4. निर्धन पुरुष ते नकी हरी जाणवो
कृष्णना तू गुण तर्जा अन्य भावे
मंत्रने तंत्र अवर आराधना
दुष्टनी संगत नित्य राखे ॥
तारा भक्त नी संगते आवे नहि
काम ने क्रोध माटे रातो
कृष्ण कथा भक्ति रहे अति वेगळो
विषय रसपान ते नित्य पीतो ॥
कृष्ण नामनो आशरो जेहने,
तेहने दोहळा दुःख न होये;
भणे नरसैयो कृष्ण गुण गाना
जन्म जन्म हरीभक्त होये ॥

Nirdhan purush te naki harī jāṇavo
Krishnana tū guṇ tarjā anya bhāvé
Mantra né tantra avar arādhanā
Dushṭani sangat nitya rākhé//
Tārā bhaktnī sangate āve nahi
Kām ne krodh māṭe rāto
Krishna katha bhakti rahe ati veglo
Vishay rasapan te nitya pito//
Krishna naamno āśaro jehne
Téhané dohlā duhkha na hoye
Bhaṇe narasaiyo krishna guṇ gātā
Janma janma haribhakt hoye//

4. Nirdhan Purush

Those who do not know Hari are poor!

They ignore Krishna's good qualities and pray to others!

They indulge in diverse forms of worship like Mantra, Tantra etc.

They every day mix with evil people

They do not mix with your devotees!

They are overwhelmed by lust and anger!

The story of Krishna is very different. One should learn its essence by praying to Him daily!

Those who chant the name of Krishna will see their sorrows disappear!

Narsi says: To be able to sing of Krishna's good qualities, one should be a devotee of God in several births!

राग : मल्हार

Rāga : Malhār

5. साधु साचे भजो चरण गोविंदना
मानवी देह ते तत्त्व कहिये
कृष्ण कहो, कृष्ण कहो वलीवल्ती कृष्ण कहो,
कृष्ण कहेना सहु सुख लहिये॥ साधु साचे

कृष्ण सेवा तणी अमर ईच्छा करे,
मूढमती मानवी कोई न जणे
कृष्णनु नाम रखे हृदये भी वीसरे
धन्य मां धन्य कृष्ण प्रमाणे॥ साधु साचे

जेने जोवा महामुनी जन वन भ्रमे,
विठ्ठलो वनमो गायो आरे
भणे नरसैयो जे चतुर नर ते खरो
अहर्निश कृष्ण श्रीकृष्ण धारे ॥ साधु साचे

Sādhu sāche bhajo charaṇ govindnā
Mānavī deh te tattv kahiye
Krishna kaho krishna kaho valīvalī krishna kaho
Krishna kahénā sahu sukh lahiye// Sādhu sāche

Krishna sevā taṇī amar īcchā kare
Mūdhmatī mānavī koī na jaṇé
Krishna nām rakhé hridayé bhi vīsaré
Dhanya mām dhanya krishna pramāṇé// Sādhu sāche

Jéné jovā mahāmunī jan van bhrame
Vidulo vanmo gāyo āré
Bhaṇe Narasaiyo je chatur nar te kharo
Aharniś krishna śrī krishna dhāré // Sādhu sāche

5. Saadhu Saache Bhajo Charan

He is called a devout person, who worships the feet of Govinda!

This is called the essence of human existence!

Chant Krishna's name again and again, with humility and devotion!

Chanting Krishna's name leads to bliss!

To serve Krishna should be the undying desire!

But foolish men do not know this!

The name of Krishna is etched on the hearts of those who are enlightened and are blessed by Him!

When sages and savants wander in forests

God comes singing all the way!

Narsi says: Those who remember Krishna day and night, are clever persons!

राग : तिलककामोद

Rāga : Tilakkāmod

6. संत करुणा थकी, सकल कारज सरे
कृष्ण करुणा थकी, कृष्ण भासे।
जगत्करुणा थकी योनि नित्य नवी धरे,
पेरे पेरे देह गर्भवासे॥
संत सुखिया सदा दुःख नवधरे कदा
जीव जंजाळ भरपूर भाता॥
जगत उन्मत्त करे विषे वासना धरे
भक्त भगवंत संघ रंग राता॥
जगत गनि परहरी, भवती ले दृढ करी
अखिल अधभर हरी दूध न जाशे।
भणे नरसैयो संत संतने सेवता
पेरेपेरे परम आनंद थाशे॥

Sant karuṇā thakī sakal kāraj sare
Krishna karuṇā thakī Krishna bhāse/
Jagatkaruṇā thakī yoni nitya navī dhare
Pere pere deh garbhvāse//
Sant sukhiyā sadā duhkh navadhare kadā
Jīv janjaal bharpūr bhātā//
Jagat unmatt kare vishe vāsanā dharé
Bhakt bhagavant sangh rang rātā//
Jagat gati parharī bhavati le dridh karī
Akhil adhbhar hari dudh na jāśe/
Bhaṇé Narasaiyo sant santne sevta
Pérépéré param ānand thāśe//

6. Sant Karuna

The kindness of saints helps us in all our work.

The kindness of Krishna helps us to see Krishna!

The kindness of the world helps us in getting rebirth and new bodies from new wombs!

Saints are always happy, they never succumb to sorrow, though worldly life is full of problems!

The arrogant world falls prey to sensory vices.

But devotees of the Lord are engrossed in thoughts about the Lord!

When good people focus on God and firmly believe in Him, their sins get washed away!

Narsi says: When a saint meets another saint, extreme joy and bliss result.

राग : सोहनी

Rāga : Sohani

7. हरिनाम विना नर सूतकी, एने अडवानो अधिकार नही
प्रभु तजी अंवर उपासे जे धिक धिक तेनो अवतार सही॥
हरि रंगे रातो रहे गुण गातो, करतो गोविंद गुण गान रे।
प्रेम भवती रसमग्न शामनु, निशदिन धरतो ध्यान रे॥
तप करे तीरथ कोटि करे कोई, नहि आवे ते तोले रे।
भणे नरसैयो धन्य, धन्य श्रीरामकृष्ण मुख बोले रे॥

Hari nām vinā nar sutkī yene aḍvāno adhikār nahī
Prabhu tajī avar upaseje dhik dhik teno avatār sahī//
Harī rangé rāto rahé guṇ gato karto govind guṇ gān ré/
Prem bhavati rasmagn śaamnu niśadin dharto dhyān ré//
Tap kare tīrath koṭi kare koyī nahi āve te toḷe ré/
Bhaṇe Narasaiyo dhanya, dhanya Shri Ramkrishna mukh bole re//

7. Harinaam vinaa

Without the chanting of Hari's name one becomes an unacceptable untouchable!

He has no right to touch or criticise anyone!

O! Lord! Those who do not pray to you and run after transient things are worthless beings!

There are, however, many who think of Hari and sing His eulogies!

Immersed in love and devotion, they pray to Him day and night!

Some indulge in penance, some go on myriad pilgrimages. They weigh and think of the illusory future!

Narasaiyā says: He is the blessed one, who constantly utters the name of Sri Ram! Sri Krishna!

राग : मिश्र पीलू Rāga : Mishra Piloo

8. जसोदाजी जमवाने तेडे, नाचना हरी आवेरे;
बोले मीठडा बोलडिया ने अंगोअंग नचावे रे ॥
मुखनी शोभा शी कहूं जाणे, पूनम चंद्र विराजे रे;
नेत्रकमलना चाला जोई जोई, मनमथ मनमां तलाजे रे ॥
अंजन् बेऊंए नयणे सार्या उर लटके गजमोती रे;
तिलकतणी रेखा अति सुंदर, माता हरखे जोती रे ॥
स्नेह जणावी ने पुत्र ने भार्यो, अवीने कोटे वळ्य्यो रे;
लाडकडो अति लाडकरे छे, क्षण ना मेलू अलगो रे ॥
खोले बेसाडीने भोजन करता, माता आनंद पाई रे;
भक्तवत्सल भूधरजी मल्या, महेता नरसैयोनो स्वामी रे ॥

Jasodājī jamwāne teḍe nāchnā harī āvé ré
Bole mīṭhḍā bolḍiyā ne ango ang nachāvé ré//
Mukhnī śobhā śi kahūn jāṇe poonam chandra virāje ré
Netrkamalnā chala joī manmath manamā talājé ré//
Anjan beuneh nayne sāryā ur latke gajmoti ré
Tilaktani rekhā ati sundar mātā harkhe joti ré//
Snehjaṇāvī ne putrane bhāryo a āvīne kote vaḷayyó ré
Lāḍakḍo ati ladkare chhe kshan na melu alago re//
Khole besādī ne bhojan kartā mātā ānand pāyī ré
Bhaktavatsal bhudharji malya maheta narasaiyo no
Swāmī-ré//

8. Jasodaaji jamvaane

When mother Yasoda calls Krishna to eat, Hari comes to her dancing!

His sweet baby talk is more delightful, because He dances, moving every limb of the body!

The glow on His face is like that of the full moon shining in the sky!

Watching the flutter of His lotuslike eyes, even Cupid is captivated!

The collyrium is laid on both His eyes! The big pearl pendant sways with the chain, on his chest!

The *kumkum* mark on His forehead is very beautiful! And the mother looks at Him with love and admiration!

The precious pet is so pampered that he cannot be left alone even for a second!

Hari sits on His mother's lap and eats, the mother enjoys bliss in feeding Him!

Krishna's love for His devotees is like the mother's love for her child!

This protective and kind God is Narsi's Lord!

राग : जोगकंस/भीमपलास Rāga : Jogkauns/Bhimpalās

9. संसार नो भय निकट न आवे, श्रीकृष्ण गोविन्द गोपाल गाता।
उगर्यो परिक्षित श्रवणे सुनता, ताल वेणा विष्णुना गुण गाता॥
बालक ध्रुव दृढ भक्ति जाणी अविचल पदवी आपी।
असुर प्रहलादने उगारी लीधो, जनम जनमनी जडना कापी॥
देवना देवनू कृष्ण आदि देवा, तारुं नाम लेना अभे पद दाता।
ते(म) तारा नामने नरसैयो निज जपे सारकर सारकर विश्वख्याता॥

Samsār no bhay nikaṭ na āve Śrikrishna govind gopāl gātā
Ugaryon Parikshit śravaṇe sunta tāḷ veṇā vishṇu guṇ gātā
Bālak Dhruv dridh bhakti jāṇi avichal padvī api
Asur Prahlādné ugārī līdho janam janamni jad to kapi
Devnā devan krishna ādidévā tārun nām lenā abhé pad dātā
Te(ma) tārā nāmne Narasaiyo nij jape saarkar saarkar viśvakhyātā

9. Samsarano bhay

The fear of Samsara does not come near you, when you sing of Sri Krishna! Govinda! Gopala!

Parikshit was saved even in the womb, since he listened to singing of God's name, though without rhythm.

Young Dhruva, because of his firm faith in the Lord, attained the fixed, immortal status of the Pole Star!

Young Prahlada, though persecuted by his father, kept on reciting the Lord's name and attained liberation!

O! Krishna! You are the God of gods! When I recite your name, I get protection from all evil.

Narsi chants your name daily, as that is the worldfamous, easy path of prayer!

राग : मिश्र खमाज़ Rāga : Mishra Khamās

10. वैष्णव जनने विषय भी टलवु हरवुं मांही हो भी मन रे
इंन्द्रिय कोई अपवाद करे नही तेने कहिये वैष्णव जन रे॥
कृष्ण कृष्ण कहेता कंठसी सुके, तोये न मुके निज नाम रे
श्वासो श्वासे समरे श्रीहरी, मन न व्यापे काम रे॥
अंतर वृत्ति अखंड राखें हरीशु, धरे कृष्णनु ध्यान रे
व्रजवासीनी लीला उपासे, बीजु सुणे नही कान रे॥
जगशु तोडे न जोडे प्रभुशु जगशु जोडे प्रभुशु त्रुटीरे
तेने कोई वैष्णव न कहेशो, जमडा लई जाशे कुटीरे॥
कृष्ण विना कोई अन्य न देखे, जेनी वृत्ति छे कृष्णाकार रे
वैष्णव कहावे ने विषय न जाणे, तेने वारंवार धिक्कार रे॥

Vaishnav janane vishay bhi talavu haravu mahi hobhī man ré
Indriya koī apavād kare nahī tene kahiye vaishnav jan ré
Krishna krishna kaheta kanṭhsi suke, toyé na muké nij nām ré
Śwāso śwāse samre śrīharī man na vyāpé kām ré
Antar vritti akhaṇḍ rākhe harīśu chare krishnanu dhyān ré
Vrajvāsīnī līlā upāse bīju suṇé nahī kān ré
Jagaśu toḍe na joḍé prabhuśu jagaśu joḍé prabhuśu truti ré
Tene koi vaishnav na kaheśo, jamda layi jāśe kuṭī ré
Krishna vinā kói anya na dékhé jéni vritti cché krishnākār ré
Vaishnav kahāve ne vishay na jāṇe, tene vāramvār dhikkār ré

10. Vaishnav janane

Those who avoid bad qualities, have a pure and sympathetic heart,

Whose senses do not go astray can really be called men of God!

Chanting the name of Krishna, their throats become dry, but they do not stop their prayers!

In every breath, they remember God and their minds do not waver!

Their innermost thoughts are only on Hari and they think only of Krishna!

The devotees of Brindavan do not hear anything other than Krishna's name!

Those who indulge in violence and terrorism in this world find fault with God!

No one calls them men of God, they die violent and painful deaths! Some others do not see anything other than Krishna, their thoughts only centre round Krishna!

Those who call themselves men of God and indulge in vices should be condemned!

SONGS OF ANNAMACHARYA

(15th-16th Century A.D.)

	Song	*Rāga*
1.	Sriman Narayana	Bhoopalam
2.	Bhavayami Balagopalam	Yamankalyan
3.	Idiye Sadhana	Ritigowla
4.	Deva devam Bhaje	Hindolam
5.	Cheri Yasodakku Sissu	Mohanam
6.	Dolayam	Khamas
7.	Jo Achyuta Ananta Jo Jo Mukunda	Kafi
8.	Okapari Kokapari	Kharaharapriya
9.	Bhavamulona	Suddha Dhanyasi
10.	Nee Naamame	Madhyamavati

ANNAMACHARYA

ANNAMACHARYA (1424-1503 A.D.)

Annamacharya, one of the greatest Telugu poets and a great devotee of Sri Venkateswara of Tirupati, was born in 1424 A.D. in Tallapaaka, a village in Cuddapah district of Andhra Pradesh, India. He lived upto the ripe old age of 79 years, dying in 1503 A.D.

The Deity in Tirupati was Annamacharya's obsession from a young age. He ran to Tirupati from his village and the first *darsan* of the Lord of Tirupati was an ecstatic experience for him and made him burst into devotional songs in praise of his chosen Deity.

Most of Annamacharya's songs centre round Lord Venkateswara of Tirupati. To him the Lord was most accessible. He prays to Him, praises Him, talks with Him, argues with Him, quarrels with Him, pleads for His grace and surrenders to Him.

Annamacharya's *samkirtanas* or songs of praise of the Lord had a profound influence on Purandharadasa, who was a contemporary of Annamacharya and met him at Tirupati.

His influence is also seen in the works of the seventeenth century Telugu poet, Kshetrajna.

Devotional fervour is the main element in Annamacharya's compositions.

Like a true mystic, he came face to face with God and had a direct, immediate, firsthand, intuitive understanding of the Supreme Power, whose patent manifestation was Lord Venkateswara of Tirupati.

राग : भूपालम् Rāga : Bhūpālam

1. श्रीमन्नारायण – श्रीमन्नारायण
श्रीमन्नारायण नी – श्रीपादमे शरणु (श्रीमन्)

कमलासतीमुख कमल कमल हित
कमलप्रिया, कमलेक्षणा
कमलासनहित गरुड गमन श्री
कमलनाभ नी पद कमल मे शरणु (श्रीमन्)

परमयोगिजन भागधेय श्री
परमपुरुषा परात्परा
परमात्मा परमाणुरूप श्री
तिरुवेंकटगिरि देवा शरणु (श्रीमन्)

Śrīman nārāyaṇa - Śrīman nārāyaṇa
Śrīman nārāyaṇa nī - Śrīpādame śaraṇu (Śrīman)

Kamalāsatīmukha kamala kamala hita
Kamalapriyā kamalékṣaṇā
Kamalāsana hita garuḍa gamana Śrī
Kamalanābha nī pada kamalamé śaraṇu (Śrīman)

Paramayogijana bhāgadhéya Śrī
Paramapuruṣa parātparā
Paramātma paramāṇu rūpa Śrī
Tiruvénkata giri dévā śaraṇu (Śrīman)

1. Sreeman Narayana

O! Auspicious Lord Narayana! the abode of all beings! O! Auspicious Narayana!

Your holy feet are my refuge!

To the lotuslike face of Lakshmi you are the sun!

You are dear to Lakshmi and your glance is like the lotus (her home)!

You are dear to Brahma, who is seated on the lotus!

Your vehicle is Garuda, the King of birds!

You have the lotus on the navel!

Your lotuslike feet are my only refuge!

You dispense good fortune to the supreme sages!

You are the Supreme Person! You the Supreme of supremes!

You are the Universal Soul! You exist as the smallest atom!

O! Lord of the holy Venkata hills!

You are my refuge!

राग : यमनकल्याण Rāga : Yamankalyān

2. भावयामि गोपाल बालं मन
सेवितं तत्पदं चिन्तयेऽयं सदा (भावयामि)

कटि घटित मेखला खचित मणि घंटिका-
पटलनिनदेन विभ्राजमानं
कुटिलपद घटित संकुल सिञ्जतेन तं
चटुल नटना समुज्ज्वल विलासम् (भावयामि)

निरतकर कलित नवनीतं ब्रह्मादि
सुर निकर भावना शोभित पदं
तिरूवेंकटाचलस्थितमनुपमं हरिं
परम पुरूष गोपाल बालम् (भावयामि)

Bhāvayāmi gopāla bālam mana
Sévitam tatpadam çhintayéyam sadā (Bhāvayāmi)

Kaṭighaṭita mekhalā khachita maṇi ghaṇṭikā
Paṭalanina tena vıbhrājamānam
Kuṭilapada ghaṭita sankula sinjitena tam
Chaṭula naṭanā samujjwala vilāsam (Bhāvayāmi)

Niratakara kalita navanītam brahmādi
Sura nikara bhāvanā śobhita padam
Tiruvenkaṭāchala sthitamanupamam harim
Parama puruṣam gópāla bālam (Bhāvayāmi)

2. Bhavayami Gopala balam

I meditate on the young boy Gopala, who is to be worshipped through the mind and whose feet should always be remembered.

I meditate on the young boy Gopala who shines with the jingling gemset girdles and anklets around the bent feet which shake and jingle when he dances.

I meditate on the young boy Gopala whose hands are always besmeared with butter and whose feet shine by the worship of the multitudes of angels led by Brahma.

Who stays in the holy Venkata hills, who is peerless!

Hari, the Supreme Person, the young boy Gopala!

राग : रीतिगौळ Rāga : Rītigowḷa

3. इदिये साधनमिहपरमुमुलकुनु
पधिलमु मास्वामि परमपु नामं (इदि)

कलि दोष हरमु कैवल्यकरमु
अलरिन माश्री हरि नामं
सुलभमु सौख्यमु शोभन तिलकमु
पलुमारू श्री पति नामं (इदि)

पापनाशनमु बन्ध विमोचनमु
पैपै निदिये भूपति नामं
स्थापित धनमिदि सर्व रक्षकमु
धापुरमिदि माधव नामं (इदि)

Idiye sādhanamihaparamulakunu
Padhilamu māswāmi paramapu nāmam (idi)

Kalidoṣaharamu kaivalyakaramu
Alarina māśrī hari nāmam
Sulabhamu sowkhyamu śobhana tilakamu
Palumāru śrī pati nāmam (idi)

Pāpanāśanamu bandha vimócanamu
Paipai nidiyé bhūpati nāmam
Sthāpita dhanamidi sarva rakṣakamu
Dhāpuramidi mādhava nāmam (idi)

3. Idiye Sadhana

(Chanting) my Lord's name, the Supreme One's name is my only mode of worship, my only solace for my life here and hereafter!

My Auspicious Lord's name removes the afflictions of the Kali age, it gives salvation easily!

The name of Lakshmi's Lord is simple, accessible and most auspicious!

Again and again I sing the name of Madhava, Lakshmi's Lord and Bhoopati, the earth's Lord which destroys all sins, liberates from bondage, is the highest wealth, gives total protection and is my armour!

नेममु दीममु नित्यकर्ममिदि
तोमटि गोविन्दुनि नाममु
हेममु शरणमु इन्निट माकु
एमेरा श्री वेङ्कटेश्वरु नाममम् (इदि)

Némamu dīmamu nityakarmamidi
Tómaṭi Góvinduni nāmamu
Hémamu araṇamu innita māku
Émérā śrī Vénkateśwaru nāmam (idi)

The Lord's name is my code of conduct, virtue, the discharge of my daily duties.

The name of Govinda is chanted by groups of devotees.

The name of Lord Venkateswara is, in every way, the ultimate goal and always my succour.

राग : हिन्दोळम् Rāga : Hindolam

4. देव देवं भजे दिव्य प्रभावम्
रावणासुर वैरि रघुपुङ्गवं (देव)

राजवरशेखरं रविकुलसुधाकरम्
आजानुबाहु नीलाभ्रकायम्
राजारिकोदण्ड राजदीक्ष गुरुम्
राजीवलोचनं रामचन्द्रम् (देव)

Deva Devam bhaje divyaprabhāvam
Rāvaṇāsura vairi raghu puṅgavam (Deva)

Rājavara śekharam Ravikulasudhākaram
Ājānubāhu nīlābhrakāyam
Rājāri kodaṇḍa rājadīkṣā gurum
Rajīvalochanam Rāmachandram (Deva)

4. Deva devam Bhaje

I worship the omnipotent God of gods,
the enemy of the demon Ravana
Rama, the Scion of the Raghu race.

I worship the Supreme Narayana, worshipped by Brahma
Who broke the bow of Siva acquired by Janaka
Who liberated Lanka and protected Vibhishana
Rama, who is Venkatesa, worshipped by sages and learned persons.

I worship:
the King of kings, who is the diadem of the Surya clan
Who has long arms and whose body is bluehued like the clouds
Who holds the Kodanda bow to destroy enemies and is the teacher in kingly conduct
Ramachandra, whose eyes are like lotuses.

नीलाजीमूत सन्निभ शरीरं घनवि-
शालवक्षं विमल जलजनाभम्
तालाहिनगहरं धर्म संस्थापनम्
भूललनाधिपं भोगि शयनम् (देव)

पंकजासन विनतु परम नारायणम्
शंकरार्जित जनक चाप दळनम्
लंका विशोषणं लालित विभीषणम्
वेंकटेशं साधु विबुध विनुतम् (देव)

Nīlajīmūta sannibha śarīram ghanavi-
Śāla vakṣam vimala jalajanābham
Tālāhi nagaharam dharma sansthāpanam
Bhūlalanādhipam bhogi śayanam (Deva)

Pankajāsana vinuta parama nārāyaṇam
Śankarārjita janaka chāpa daḷanam
Lankā viśóshaṇam lālīta vibhīshaṇam
Vénkatéśam sādhu vibudha vinutam (Deva)

I worship:

the Lord, whose strong, broad chested body resembles the blue cloud

From whose navel the pure lotus rises

Who felled the seven palm trees which looked like the hood of a serpent and who established righteousness, the Lord of Bhoodevi, Mother Earth and who lies on the serpent Adi Sesha!

I worship the Supreme Narayana (the abode of all beings), venerated by Brahma seated on the lotus

Who broke the bow of Siva, acquired by Janaka

Who liberated Lanka and protected Vibhishana,

Rama, who is Venkatesa, worshipped by the righteous and the learned ones.

राग : मोहनम् Rāga : Móhanam

5. चेरि यशोदकु शिशु वितडु
धारुणि ब्रह्मकु दण्ड्रियुनितडु (चेरि)

सोलसि शूचिननु सूर्य चन्द्रुलनु
ललिवेद जल्लडु लक्षणुडु
निलिचिन निलुवुन निखिल देवतल
कलिकिंचु सुरल गनिवो इतडु (चेरि)

Cheri yasódaku śiśu vitaḍu
Dhāruṇi brahmaku daṇḍriyunitaḍu (Cheri)

Solasi jūchinanu sūrya chandrulanu
Laliveda jalledu lakshanuḍu
Nilichina niluvuna nikhiladevatala
Kalikinchu surala ganivó itaḍu (Cheri)

5. Cheri Yasodakku

He who is the father of Brahma, the creator, became the child of Yasoda on earth.

In Him I have seen the sun and the moon!

His splendour is unparalleled!

As He stands, all the celestials are manifest!

माटलाडिननु मरियजांडमकु
कोटुलु वोडमेटि गुणरासि
नीटगु नूर्पुल निखिल वेदमुलु
चाटुव नूरेटि समुद्रमिदडु (चेरि)

मुंगिट तोलसिन मोहनमात्मल
पोंगिन्चे घन पुरुषुडु
संगीत मावंटि शरणागतुलकु
अंगमु श्री वेङ्कटाद्रिपुडिदडु (चेरि)

Māṭalādinanu mariyajāmdamaku
Koṭulu voḍameṭi guṇa rāsi
Nīṭagu nūrpula mikhila vedamulu
Chāṭuva nūreṭi samutra mitaḍu (Cheri)

Mungiṭa tólasina mohanamātmala
Ponginché ghana purushuḍu
Sangati māvamti śaraṇāgatulaku
Angamu śrī venkatādripu ḍitaḍu (Cheri)

When he opens His mouth to talk, one can see millions of universes inside Him!

All the scriptures are in Him! He is verily the ocean of knowledge!

When He appears in front of you, He fills you with great bliss.

He is close to me and all those who have sought refuge in Him.

He is the Ruler of the seven Venkata Hills!

राग : खमाज़ | Rāga : Khamās

6. डोलायां चल डोलायांम् हरे डोलायाम् (डोला)

मीन कूर्म वराह मृगपति अवतार
दानवारे गुण शौरे धरणि धर मारजनक (डोला)

वामन रामराम वरकृष्ण अवतार
श्यामलांगा रंग रंग सामजवरद मुरहरन (डोला)

दारूण बुद्ध कलिकि दशविध अवतार
सीरपाणे गोसमाणे श्रीवेङ्कटगिरि कूटनिलय (डोला)

Dólāyam chala dolāyām haré dólāyām (dolā)

Mīna kūrma varāha mrugapati avatāra
Dāmavāre guṇa śowré dharaṇidhara mārajanaka (dolā)

Vāmana rāma rāma varakriṣṇa avatāra
Śyāmalāngā ranga ranga sāmajavarada muraharana (dolā)

Dāruṇa buddha kaliki daśavidha avatāra
Sīrapāṇe gosamāṇe śrīvenkaṭagiri kūṭanilaya (dolā)

6. Dolayam

Swing and sway, O! Hari!

You, who incarnated as fish, tortoise, boar and Man-lion,

You, the enemy of demons, the embodiment of all good qualities,

O! Sauri, descendant of Sura!

Who held the earth, the father of Cupid!

Swing and sway, O! Hari!

You, who incarnated as Vamana, the dwarf, Parasurama and the supreme Krishna,

Whose body is darkhued, O! Handsome One, who saved the Elephant King and destroyed Mura, the demon!

Swing and sway, O! Hari!

You, who incarnated as the Buddha, and Kalki as well, thus in ten different forms,

O! Lord with the plough in hand, protector of all beings!

Resident of the holy Venkata hills!

Swing and sway, O! Hari!

राग : काफी

Rāga : Kāfi

7. जो अच्युतानन्द जो जो मुकुन्द
रावे परमानन्द राम गोविन्द! (जो)

नन्दु निन्टनु जेरि नयमु मिरंग
चन्द्रवदनलु नीकु सेव चेयंग
नन्दमुग वारिण्ड्ल नाडुचुण्टंग
मन्दलकु दोंग मामुट्टु रंग! (जो)

पालवाराशिलो पव्वनिञ्चनावु
मेलुगा वसुदेवुकुतयिञ्चिनावु
बालुगा मुनुलक भयमिञ्चिनावु
बालुदैयुन्दि गोपालुडैनावु (जो)

Jó achyutānanda jo jo mukunda
Rāvé paramānanda rāma góvinda! (Jo)

Nandu nintanujéri nayamu miranga
Chandravadanalu niku séva chéyanga
Nanda muga vārindla nāḍu chunṭanga
Mandalaku donga mamuṭṭuranga! (Jo)

Pālavārasilό pavvaminchināvu
Mélugā vasudevu kutayinchināvu
Bālugā munulaka bhayaminchināvu
Bāludaiyundi gópāludaināvu (Jo)

7. Jo Achyuta

My never ending joy! Mukunda!

Darling! You are the embodiment of supreme happiness! Dear Rama! Govinda! Come here!

In Nanda's house, as beautiful, moonfaced ladies serve you,

The women in the neighbourhood call you: "O! thief! Our dear, darling Ranga!"

You lie on the milky ocean!

Gloriously you were born as the son of Vasudeva!

As a child you removed the fears of the sages!

As a young boy, you became Gopala, the cowherd!

अंगजुनिकन्न मायन्न यिट्टुरारा
बंगारू गिन्नेलो पालु पोसेरा
दोंगनिवानि सतुलु पोंगुचुन्नारा
मुंगिट नाडरा मोहनाकारा (जो)

अङ्गुगाताळ्ळपाकन्नय्य चाल
शृंगार रचनगा चेप्पनीजोल
संगतिग सकल संपदल नीवेळ
मंगळमु किलुपट्ल मदनगोपाल (जो)

Angajunikanna māyanna yiṭurārā
Bangāru ginnelo pālu posérā
Donganivāni satulu ponguchunnārā
Mungita nāḍarā mohanākārā (Jo)

Angugātāllapākannaiya chāla
Śringāra rachanagā chepppanijóla
Sangatiga sakala sampadala nīveḷa
Mangaḷamu kilupaṭla madanagopāla (Jo)

My child! Father of the god of love!
You magical One! Come here!
In a golden cup I have kept milk for you!
The women are saying that you are a thief, out of spite!
O! Charming One! Come here and dance on the doorstep!

Beautifully, Tallapaka Annayya sings this lovely lullaby!
You bestow all material wealth and auspiciousness!
May good befall you!
O! Madanagopala of Kilupatla!

राग : खरहरप्रिया

Rāga : Kharaharapriyā

8. ओकपरि कोकपरि कोय्यारमै
मोकमुन कळ्ळेल्ला मोलिचि नट्लुण्डे (ओकपरि)

जगदेकपतिमेन जल्लिन कर्पूरधूलि
जिगिकोनि नलुवङ्क चिन्दगानु
मोगि चन्द्रमुखि नुरमुन निलिसे गान
पोगरु वेन्नल दिजपोसिनट्लुण्डे (ओकपरि)

Okapari kokapari koyyāramai
Mokamuna kaḷalellā molichi naṭlundé (Okapari)

Jagadékapati ména jallina karpūradhūḷi
Jigikoni naluvanka chindagānu
Mogi chandramukhi nuramuna nilisé gāna
Pogaru vennela dijaposinatlunḍé (Okapari)

8. Okapari kokapari

Each and every time I see

His face takes on new luminiscence!

As the purified camphor powder sprinkled on the body of the Lord of universe!

Liquefies and flows copiously over the moonfaced beloved on His chest,

It looks as though vibrant moonlight outlines the contours of her body!

पोरि मेरुगु जेक्कुल बूसिन तट्टुपुनुगु
करगि इरुटेसल कारगानु
करिगमन विभुडु कनुक मोहमदमु
तोरिगि सामजसिरि तोलगिनट्लुण्डे (ओकपरि)

मेरय श्री वेङ्कटेशुमेन सिंगारमुखानु
तरचयिन सोंमुलु धरियिंसगा
मेरुगुबोणि अलमेलु मंगयु दानु
मेरुपु मेघमुगूटि मेरसिनट्लुण्डे (ओकपरि)

Pori merugu jekkula būsina taṭṭupanugu
Karagi irutesala kāragānu
Karigamanavibhuḍu kanuka móhamadamu
Torigi sāmajasiri tolaginatlunḍé (Okapari)

Meraya śrī vénkaṭéśuména singāramukhānu
Tarachayina sommulu dhariyimsagā
Merugubóṇi alamélu mangayu dānu
Merupu méghamugūṭi merasinatlunḍé (Okapari)

The wet unguent (Punugu) applied to the Lord's cheeks as it melts and drips down on either side, looks like the ichor streaming down an elephant's jowls! (After all) He is the Lord of the elephantgaited Padmavati!

The dark body of Venkateswara shines by the ornaments He wears

Alamelumanga (His consort) has a naturally shining body

Together, they are like cloud and lightning lit up simultaneously!

राग : शुद्ध धन्यासि Rāga : Suddha Dhanyāsi

9. भावमुलोन बाह्यमु नन्दुनु
गोविन्द गोविन्दअनि कोलुववोमनसा (भाव)

हरि अवतारमुले अखिल देवतलु
हरि लोनिवे ब्रह्माण्डंमुलु
हरि नाममुले अन्निमन्त्रंमुलु
हरि हरि हरि हरि हरि यनवो मनसा (भाव)

Bhāvamulóna bāhyamu nandunu
Govinda govinda ani koluvavó manasā (Bhāva)

Hari avatāramulé akhila dévatalu
Harilonivé brahmāṇḍammulu
Harināmamulé anni mantrammulu
Hari hari hari hari hari yanavo manasā (Bhāva)

9. Bhavamulona

O! Mind! Chanting the name Govinda, serve the Lord,
in thought and action, both within and without.

All gods are the manifestations of Hari alone.
All the universes are within Hari!
All holy chants are Hari's name only.
Sing over and over again: Hari! Hari! Hari! Hari! O! Mind!

विष्णुनि महिमले विहित कर्ममुलु
विष्णुनि पोगडेडि वेदंबुलु
विष्णुडोक्कडे विश्वान्तरात्मुडु
विष्णुवु विष्णुवनि वेतकवो मनसा (भाव)

अच्युतुडितडे आदियुमनन्तमु
अच्युतुडे असुरान्तकुडु
अच्युतुडु श्रीवेंकटाद्रि मदिनिदे
अच्युत अच्युत शरणनवो मनसा (भाव)

Vishṇuni mahimalé vihita karmamulu
Vishṇuni pogaḍeḍi vedambulu
Vishṇu ḍokkaḍe visvāntarātmudu
Vishṇuvuviṣṇuvani vetakavo manasā (Bhāva)

Achyu tuḍitadé ādiyumanantamu
Achyutuḍe asurāntakuḍu
Achyutuḍu śrī vénkaṭadri mīdanidé
Achyuta achyuta śaraṇanavó manasā (Bhāva)

All the duties we do are by His greatness!
His praises are the Vedas.
Vishnu is the Universal Soul.
O! Mind! Search for Him, chanting his name: Vishnu, Vishnu!

He, the Eternal One, Achyuta is the beginning and the end.
He, Achyuta, is the destroyer of demons.
He, Achyuta, is here on the Venkata hills.
O! Mind! seek refuge in His name: Achyuta!

राग : मध्यमावती Rāga : Madhyamāvati

10. नी नाममे माकु निधियु निधानमु
नी नाममे आत्म निधानमु जनमु (नी)

नमो नमो केशव नमो नारायणा
नमो नमो माधव नमो गोविन्दा
नमो नमो विष्णु नमो मधुसूदन
नमो त्रिविक्रम नमो वामन (नी)

Nī nāmamé māku nidhiyu nidhānamu
Nī nāmamé ātma nidhānamu janamu (Nī)

Namó namó keśava namó nārāyaṇā
Namó namó mādhava namó govindā
Namó namó vishnu namó madhusūdana
Namó trivikrama namo vāmana (Nī)

नामे नमो श्रीधर नमो हृषीकेश
नमो पद्मनाभ नमो दामोदर
नमो संकर्षण नमो वासुदेव
नमो प्रद्युम्न नमो अनिरुद्ध (नी)

Namó namó śrīdhara namó hrishīkéśa
Namó padmanābha namó dāmodara
Namó sankarshaṇa namó vāsudeva
Namó pradyumna namó aniruddha (Nī)

10. Nee naamame

Your name alone is our treasure, support!

Your name alone is the means to self-realisation!

Prostrations to you, O! Kesava! O! Narayana!

Prostrations again and again to you, O! Madhava, Lord of Lakshmi! O! Govinda, who can be known through scriptures!

Prostrations to you, O! Madhusudana, the destroyer of the demon Madhu!

Prostrations to you, O! Trivikrama, the Victorious One!

Prostrations to you, O! Vamana!

Prostrations again and again to Sreedhara, the Holder of Lakshmi! O! Hrishikesa!

Prostrations to you, O! Padmanabha! O! Damodara!

Prostrations to you, O! Sankarshana! O! Vasudeva!

Prostrations to you, O! Pradyumna! O! Aniruddha!

Note: The various epithets used by Sri Annamacharya in addressing the Lord are familiar names of Vishnu; the meaning of some of the rarer names is given below:

Hrishikesa = Master of the senses
Damodara = One who has a benevolent, self-controlled mind
Pradyumna = One whose wealth is of a superior order
Sankarshana = One who attracts
Aniruddha = One who has not been obstructed by anyone

नमो पुरुषोत्तम नमो अधोक्षज
नमो नरसिंह नमोस्तु अच्युत
नमो जनार्दन नमोस्तु उपेन्द्र
नमो श्री वेंकटेश नमो श्री कृष्ण (नी)

Namó purushóttama namó adhókshaja
Namó narasimha namóstu achyuta
Namó janārdana namóstu upendra
Namó srī vénkaṭéśa namó śrī krishṇa (Nī)

Prostrations to you, O! Purushottama, the Supreme of persons! O! Adhokshaja!

Prostrations to you, O! Narasimha, Man-lion! O! Achyuta, the Eternal One!

Prostrations to you, O! Janardana! O! Upendra!

Prostrations to you, O! Auspicious Lord Venkateswara! O! Sree Krishna!

Adhokshaja = Unknowable by direct perception
Janardana = One who tries people or one to whom all devotees pray for success and salvation
Upendra = One who is greater than Indra

SONGS OF SYAMA SASTRI

(18th-19th Century A.D.)

	Song	*Rāga*
1.	Sarojadalanetri	Sankarabharanam
2.	Karuna juda	Sri
3.	Trilokamata	Paras
4.	Ninnu vina	Poorvikalyani
5.	Maayamma	Ahiri
6.	O! Jagadamba	Ananda Bhairavi
7.	Nannu brovu	Lalita
8.	Kamakshi	Varali
9.	Birana Varalinchi	Kalyani
10.	Paalinchu Kamakshi	Madhyamavati

SYAMA SASTRI

SYAMA SASTRI (26 April 1762-6 February 1827 A.D.)

Syama Sastri is the eldest of the Trinity of Carnatic music-saints, the other two being Muthuswami Dikshitar and Tyagaraja.

Syama Sastri was born at Tiruvarur, but went to Thanjavur at the age of nineteen and settled down there.

Syama Sastri was born in a family, members of which were worshippers of the Divine Mother for generations. Devotion to Divine Mother was hence part of his bloodstream. Even from an early age, he used to go to the Bangaru Kamakshi temple in Thanjavur and pour out his devotion. Music became the medium for the expression of his devotion.

All of Syama Sastri's songs centre around his favourite Deity: Kamakshi, the Divine Mother. He deemed himself as Her child. His musical compositions hence are marked by not only intense devotion, but also the spontaneity, simplicity and sincerity of a child addressing its mother.

Nadopasana or practice of music with devotion is an accepted means of God realisation and Syama Sastri, like the other two members of the trinity: Tyagaraja and Muthuswami Dikshitar, proved through his life and work how simple and effective this could be.

राग : शङ्कराभरणम् Rāga : Sankarābharaṇam

1. सरोजदळ नेत्रि हिम-गिरि-पुत्री
नी पादाम्बुजमुले
सदा नम्मिनानम्म शुभमिम्
मा श्री मीनाक्षम्मा

Saroja daḷa nétri himagiri putrī
Nī pādāmbujamulé
Sadā namminānamma śubhamim
Mā Śrī mīnakshamma

पराकुसेयक वर-दायकीनी
वले दैवमुलोकमुलो गलदा
पुराणी शुकपाणी मधुकर-वे-
णी सदाशिवुनिकि-राणी

Parakuséyaka vara dāyakīnī
Valé daivamu lokamulo galadā
Purāṇī śukapāṇī madhukara-vé
Ṇī sadāśivuniki-rāṇī

कोरिवच्चिन-वारिकेल्लनु
कीर्केलोसगे बिरुदुगदा अति
भारमा नन्नु ब्रोव तल्लि कृ-
पाल-वाल ताळ जालेने

Kórivachchina vārikellanu
Kórkelosagé birudugadā ati
Bhāramā nannu bróva talli kri-
Pāla vāla tāḷa jālené

1. Sarojadalanetri

O! Mother whose eyes are like lotus petals!

O! Daughter of the snowy mountain!

In your lotus feet I have always held faith!

Bestow me auspicious welfare! O! Mother Meenakshi, O! Fish-eyed One!

O! Granter of boons! Do not be averse to me!

Is there a Deity like you in this world?

You are the Ancient One! You hold the parrot in your hand!

Your tresses resemble bees!

You are the Queen of the ever-auspicious Lord!

You grant boons to those who beseech you!

This is your reputation!

Is protecting me such a heavy burden?

O! Merciful Mother! I cannot bear any longer.

इन्दु-मुखी करुणिंच-मनि निनु
नेन्त वेडु-कोण्टिन ना-
यन्दु जागेल-नम्मा मरि
याद-गादु दयावती नीवु

Indumukhī karuṇincha mani ninu
Nenta veḍukoṇṭini nā-
Yandu jāgélanammā mari
Yāda gāda dayāvatī nīvu

सामगान-विनोदिनी गुण-
धाम श्यामकृष्ण-नुता शुक
श्यामळा-देवी नीवेगति रति
काम-काम्य काववे नन्नु

Sāmagāna vinodinī guṇa
Dhāma śyāmakrishṇa nutā śuka
Śyāmaḷā devi nīvegati rati
Kāma kāmya kāvavé nannu

O! Moonfaced One! How many times have I prayed to you to shower mercy on me!

Why do you delay? This is not fair!

You are the merciful One!

You delight in Sama songs!

You are the treasurehouse of virtues!

The darkhued Krishna worships you!

O! Darkhued Goddess with the parrot! You are my only refuge!

You are sought after by Cupid and his wife Rati.

Please protect me!

राग : श्री Rāga : Srī

2. करुणजूड निन्नु नाम्मिन-वाडनु-
गदा इन्त पराकेल नम्मा

सरसिजासन-माधव-सन्नुत
चरणा बृहन्नायकि वेगमे

Karuṇajūda ninnu nammina-vāḍanu-
Gadā inta parākela nammā

Sarasijāsana-mādhava-sannuta
Charaṇā bruhannāyaki végamé

दीन-जनावन-मूर्तिवि नीवनि
नेनु निन्नु नेरनाम्मितिनि
गान-विनोदिनि घननिभवेणि
कामितफलदा समयमिदे

Dīna-janāvana-murtivi nīvani
Nénu ninnu neranammitini
Gāna vinodini ghana-nibha-véṇi
Kāmita phaladā samayamidé

2. Karuna juda

Look at me with kindness! I have always trusted in you!

Why this indifference? O! Mother!

Your feet are worshipped by Brahma, the lotus-seated One and Vishnu, the Lord of Lakshmi!

You are the Great Chief! Hurry (to look at me with kindness).

You are the refuge of the afflicted!

I have unflinchingly trusted in you!

You delight in music! your hair resembles the cloud!

You grant the result desired! This is the time (for you to act)!

नी महिमातिशयम्बुलनु नेन्तनि
ने जेप्पुदुनो ललिता
हेमपाङ्गि हिमगिरि-पुत्रि म-
हेश्वरि गिरीश-रमणि नी

Nī mahimātiśayambulanu nentani
Né jeppuduno lalitā
Hemapāngi himagiri putri ma-
Heśwari girīśa-ramaṇi nī

श्यामकृष्ण-परिपालिनि शूलिनि
सामज-गमना कुन्द-रदना
तामसम्बु इडुसेयक ना परि-
तापमुलनु परिहरिञ्चिन नीवु

Śyāmakrishṇa-paripālini śūlini
Sāmaja-gamana kunda-radanā
Tāmasamba iḍuséyaka nā pari-
Tāpamulanu pariharinchina nivu

How can I praise your wondrous greatness? O! Playful One!

You are golden limbed! You are the daughter of the snowy Mountain!

You are the Great Goddess! You are the Beloved of Siva, the Lord of mountains!

O! Protector of this Syamakrishna! O! Tridentholder!

Your gait is like that of the elephant! Your teeth are like jasmines!

Do not delay anymore!

Remove all my afflictions!

राग : परश् Rāga : Paras

3. त्रिलोक-माता नन्नुब्रोवु करुणनु
दिन-दिन-मिकनु ब्रोवुमु अम्बा
विलोकिम्पुमु सदय नन्नु चल्लनि
वीक्षञ्चि क्षणमुन कामाक्षि

Triloka mātā nannubrovu karuṇanu
Dina dina mikanu brovumu ambā
Vilókimpumu sadaya nannu challani
Vīkshinchi kshaṇamuna kāmākshi

निनु नम्मियुण्डग श्रम-पडवलेना
ने नेन्दुगन दिक्कु निन्नु विना
घनमुगा कोरिकल कोरिकोरियेमि-
गानक खिन्नडनैति धन्युजेसि

Ninu nammiyuṇḍaga śrama paḍavalenā
Né nendugana dikku ninnu vinā
Ghanamugā korikila korikori yemi-
Gānaka khinnaḍanaiti dhanyujési

3. Trilokamata

O! Mother of the three worlds! Show compassion and protect me!

O! Mother! Hereafter protect me everyday!

Look at me with compassion and tenderness, O! Kamakshi, whose eyes exude love!

Why should I suffer, when I trust in you?

Where can I seek refuge except in you?

Beseeching you again and again, I am despairing.

Please be merciful to me!

जपमुलेरुगनु तपमु-लेरुगनु
चपल-चित्तुडनु सततमु कृपकु
पात्रुडनु वेडेदनु निनु
कीर्तिञ्चि येट्लैन नी बिड्डयनि

Japamaleruganu tapamuleruganu
Chapala chittuḍanu satatamu kripaku
Pātruḍanu véḍadana ninu
Kīrtinchi yeṭlaina nī biḍḍayani

मरुवक निनु ने मदि तलचगनु
मन्निञ्चि वेरवकुमन रादा
शरणमे सुजनुलपालि कल्पकवल्ली
शङ्करी श्यामकृष्णसोदरी

Maruvaka ninu né madi talacaganu
Manninchi veravakumana rādā
Śaraṇamé sujanulapāli kalpakavallī
Śankarī śyāmakriṣṇa sódarī

I do not do Japa or tapa (I do not chant nor do penance). I am of a wavering mind!

Desiring that I should receive your grace, as your child I praise you.

Without ever forgetting, I always think of you!

Excuse me, can't you tell me not to be afraid?

To those good and wise persons who seek refuge in you, you grant all desires like the Kalpaka creeper!

You are Sankari, the Creatrix of good!

You are the sister of the darkhued Krishna!

राग : पूर्वीकल्याणी Rāga : Poorvikalyāni

4. निन्नु-विनाग-मरि दिक्केवरुन्नारु
निखिल लोक जननी नन्नुब्रोचुटकु

पन्नग-भूषणु-डैन काञ्चि एकाम्र-
पति-मनोहारिणी श्रीकामाक्षी

Ninnu vināga mari dikkevarunnāru
Nikhila loka jananī nannubróchuṭaku

Pannaga bhūshaṇu ḍaina kānchi yékāmra-
Pati manohāriṇī śrīkāmākshī

परम-लोभुलनु पोगडि पोगडि यति
पामरुडै तिरिगि तिरिगि वेसारि
स्थिरमुलेक अति-चपलुडैति ना-
चिन्त-दीर्चि वेवेगमे ब्रोचुटकु

Parama lóbhulanu pogaḍi pogaḍi yati
Pāmaruḍai tirigi tirigi vésāri
Sthiramuléka ati chapaludaiti nā-
chinta dīrchi vévégamé brochutaku

4. Ninnu vina

Excepting you, who is my refuge?

O! Mother of the entire universe! Who is there to protect me (except you)?

You have stolen the heart of Ekamresvara of Kanchi!

O! Auspicious Love-eyed One! O! Sree Kamakshi!

I have praised the extremely greedy ones, again and again!

I have become depressed, moving with the most depraved persons again and again!

My unsteady thoughts greedy to gain, have to be speedily stilled. Who is there to save me except you?

इललू नी-वलनेगदा नी-महिम-
येन्तनि योजिम्प येव्वरितरमु
पलुकग वशमा आदि-शेषनु कैननु
पतित-पावनी नन्नु ब्रोचुटकु

Italu nī valanegadā nī mahima-
yentani yójimpa yevvari taramu
Palukaga vaśama ādiśeshanu kainanu
Patita pāvanī nannu brochutaku

तामस-मिटुल सेय-रादिकनु
तल्लि नामोर-विनरादा दय-लेदा
कामितार्थ-फलदायकी ललिता
श्यामकृष्ण-सोदरी ब्रोचुटकु

Tāmasamiṭula seyarādikanu
Talli nāmora vinarādā daya ledā
Kāmitārtha phaladāyakī lalitā
Śyāma Krishṇa sódarī bróchutaku

These worlds exist because of you!

Who can measure your greatness?

Can even Adi Sesha, the Serpent King, describe it?

O! Purifier of the polluted! Who is there to save me except you?

Do not delay any longer!

O! Mother! Can't you hear my pleadings? Have you no compassion?

You give the fruits of desires! You are Lalita, the Playful One!

You are the sister of the darkhued Krishna!

Who is there to save me except you?

राग : आहिरि Rāga : Āhiri

5. मायम्मा-यनि ने पिलचिते
माट्लाडरादा (नातो) अम्बा
न्यायमा (मीनाक्षम्मा) मीनाक्षिकिदि
निन्नु विना वेरे दिक्केवरु-न्नारु

Māyammā-yani né pilachité
Mātlaḍarada (nató) ambā

Nyāyamā (mīnākshamma) mīnākshikidi
Ninnu vina véré dikkeverunnāru

सरसिजभव-हरि-हरनुत-सुललित-
नीपद-पङ्कजमुल
स्थिरमनि नम्मिति नम्मिति नाम्मितिनि
करुणजूडवे कात्यायनि काळिका भवानि
परमेश्वरि सुन्दरेशु-राणि बालाम्बा मधुर-वाणि

Sarasija bhava hari haranuta sulalita
Nīpada pankajamula
Sthiramani nammiti nammiti nammitini
Karuṇa jūḍavé kātyayani kāḷikā bhavāni
Paraméśwari sundaréśu rāṇi bālāmbā madhura vāni

5. Māyamma

"O! My Mother!" I call you and pray to you.

Yet, you don't talk to me. Why? Mother!

Is this just, O! Mother Meenakshi?

Excepting you, who else is my refuge?

Brahma, Vishnu and Rudra bow down at your tender lotus feet!

I firmly trust, trust, trust (in them).

Show mercy to me! O! Kaatyaayani! O! Kaalika, the dark One! O! Bhavani, Creatrix!

You are the Supreme Goddess! You are the Queen of Sundaresa!

You are Balamba, the young Mother! You are sweetspoken!

विनुत जन पाप विमोचनि ओ जन-
नी घन-नील-वेणि
विदळित-दानव-मण्डल-शमनी
वनज लोचना सुधाकराननना वरदायकि
अनयमु निनु कोरियुन्नानम्मा बङ्गारु बोम्मा

Vinuta jana pāpa vimochani o jana-
nī ghana nīla veni
Vidaḷita dānava maṇḍala samanī
Vanajalochanā sudhākarānanā varadāyaki
Anayamu ninu kóriyunnānamma bangāruvommā

अभय-मोसगि नन्नु ब्रोवुमु ओ वर-
दा निर-दातवु-गदा
अम्बिका बिड्डपै गोप्पग दय-रादा
अखिल-लोक जननी अनाथरक्षकि अनेटि बिरुदु-गादा
वैभवमु गल श्यामकृष्णसोदरि वी-शक्ति त्रिपुर-सुन्दरि

Abhaya mosagi nannubrovumu o vara-
dā nira dātavu gadā
Ambikā biḍḍapai goppaga daya rādā
Akhila loka janani anātharakshaki aneṭi birudu-gādā
Vaibhavamu gala śyāmakrishṇa sódari vī śakti tripura sundari

Those who bow down to you, you liberate from sins.

O! Mother! Whose tresses are dark blue like clouds!

You destroyed hordes of demons!

You are lotuseyed, Moonfaced, granter of boons!

O! Mother! O! Bangaru Deity! I always long for you!

Secure me from fear and protect me, O! Giver of boons!

Verily, you give in plenty!

O! Mother! Can't you shower mercy on your child?

O! Mother of all the worlds! From ancient times you have the reputation of being the saviour of the orphaned!

O! Sister of the darkhued Krishna! O! all powerful!

Tripura Sundari! the Most beauteous in the three worlds!

राग : आनन्द भैरवि Rāga : Ānanda Bhairavi

6. ओ जगदंब ननु अम्ब नी-
वु जवमुन ब्रोवु अम्ब

ई जगति गतियौ जनुलकु मरितेजमुन राजविनुत यौ-
राजकमुखि सरोजनयन सुगुणराज राजित कामाक्षि

कन्नतल्लि नादु चेन्तनिन्त
कन्नडसलुपगतगुना
निन्नु ने नम्मियुन्नवाडुगदा
नन्नोकनि ब्रोचुट करुदा
अन्निभुवनम्बुलु गाचेवु प्र-
सन्नमूर्ती अन्नपूर्णवरदा
विन्नपम्बु विन्नविञ्चि सन्निधि वि-
पन्नभयविमोचन धौरेय

Ó jagadamba nanu amba nī-
vu javamuna bróvu amba
Ī jagati gatiyau janulaku maritéjamuna rājavinuta yau-
Rājamukhi sarójanayana suguṇaraja rājita kāmākshi
Kannatalli nādu chéntaninta
Kannada salupa gata gunā
Ninnune nammi yunna vāḍugadā
Nannokani brochuṭa karudā
Annibhuvanambulu gācheva pra-
Sannamūrtī annapūrna varadā
Vinnapambu vinnavinchi sannidhi vi-
panna bhayavimóchana dhauréya

6. O! Jagadamba

O! Mother of the universe! O! Mother!

Save me fast, O! Mother!

In this universe, you are the refuge of all beings!

Your face shines with radiance! O! Lotuseyed Kamakshi, the paragon of all good qualities!

O! Mother who gave me birth! Is it right on your part to torture me?

Don't I have implicit trust in you?

Is this how you protect me? O! Protector of the universe!

You have a pleasing form! You are the granter of boons aplenty!

Listen to my prayer! O! granter of liberation to those who come to your sanctum sanctorum! You free them from all fears!

जाल मेल शैलबाल ताळ
जालनु जननी निन्नु विना
पालनाथ मुग वेरे दैवमुल
लोलमतियै नम्मितिना
नीलनुता शीलमु ने नेच्चट
नैनगान गानलोलहृदया
नीलकण्ठराणी निन्नु नम्मितिनि
निजम्बुग बलिकेदि दयचेसि

Jālamela sailabāla tāḷa-
Jālanu jananī ninnuvinā
Pālanātha muga véré daivamula
Lola matiyai nammitina
Nīlanuthā sīlamu ne nechchaṭa
Nainagāna gānalolahrudayā
Nīlakanṭharāṇī ninnu nammitini
Nijambuga balikedi dayachési

Why this deception? O! Daughter of the mountain!

I cannot stand this, O! Mother!

Is there any god, other than you, who can save me?

Have I trusted you with a wavering mind?

You are venerated by Siva! I shall sing my songs, since your heart is moved by music! O! Queen of Neelakanta, the blue- throated Lord Siva! I trust in you implicitly.

Do you lose anything in showing mercy to me?

चंचलात्मुडेनु येमि पूर्व-
सञ्चितमुल सलिपितिनो
कञ्चिकामाक्षी नेनु निन्नु पोड-
काञ्चितिनि शरणु शरणु नी
विञ्चुकाचञ्चलगति नादेस-
नुञ्चवम्मा श्यामकृष्णविनुता
मञ्चिकीर्ति निच्चुनट्टिदेविमन्-
निञ्चि नाद पराधमुल सहिञ्चि

Chanchalātmuḍenu yemi pūrva-
Sanchitamula salipitino
Kanchikāmākshī nenu ninnu poḍa
Kānchitini śaraṇu śaraṇu nī
Vinchukāchanchala gati nādesa-
Nunchavamma śyāmakrishṇa vinutā
Manchikīrti nicheunaṭṭi deviman-
Ninchi nāda parādhamula sahinchi

वरसितगिरि-निलयुनि-प्रियप्रणयिनि
पराशक्ति मनविनि विनुमा
मरियाद लेरुगनि दुष्प्रभुल
कोरि विनुतिम्पग वरं बोसगि

Varasitagiri-nilayuni-priyapraṇayini
Parāśakti manavini vinumā
Mariyāda lérugani duṣprabhula
Kori vinutimpaga varam bosagi

My mind is unsteady! I do not know what I have done in my previous births!

O! Love-eyed Goddess of Kanchi! Kamakshi! Now that I have found you, I seek refuge in you!

Continue to shower grace on me!

O! Goddess worshipped by the darkhued Krishna!

O! Goddess! give me fame and name!

Forgive me and bear with my faults!

O! Beloved of the Lord who loves to reside in the snowy mountains! O! Supreme Power! Hear my prayer!

Grant me the boon that I should not seek any favours from the wicked and the disrespectful wealthy ones!

राग : ललित Rāga : Lalita

7. ननु ब्रोवु ललिता वेगमे चाल
निन्नु नेर नम्मि-युन्न-वाडुगदा भक्त-कल्पक-लता

निन्नु विना येवरुन्नारुमागतिजन-
नी मा-जननी अतिवेगमे

Nanu brova lalitā végamé chāla
Ninnu nera nammiyunna vadugadā bhakta kalpaka latā

Ninnu vina yevarunnāru māgatijana-
Nī mā jananī ativégame

पराकु-सेयकने वच्चि कृप-सलु
प-रादा मोर-विनका
पराशक्ति गीर्वाण वन्दित-
पदानी-भक्तुडनम्मा सन्ततमु

Parāku seyakane vachchi kripa salu
Pa rādā moravinavā
Parāśakti gīrvāṇa vandita
Padā nī bhaktuḍanammā santatamu

7. Nannu brovu Lalita

O! Lalita! the playful Goddess! Save me soon!

Do I not trust in you? O! Goddess who fulfil the desires of devotees like the Kalpaka creeper!

Excepting you who else is my refuge? O! Mother! You are my mother, so save me very soon!

Do not ignore me! Can't you come and show mercy?

Can't you hear my prayers?

O! Supreme Power! Your feet are worshipped by the celestials. I am ever your devotee!

(So save me soon!)

सरोजभव-कमलनाथ-शङ्कर-
सुरेन्द्रनुत-चरिता
पुराणी-वाणी-इन्द्राणी-वन्ति
त राणी अहि भूषणुनि-राणी

Sarója bhava kamala nātha śankara
Surendra nuta charitā
Purāṇī vāṇī indrāṇī vanti-
Ta rāṇī ahi bhūṣaṇuni-rāṇī

मदात्मुलैन दुरात्म-जनुलनु
कथलनु पोगडि पोगडि
सदा ने वराल चुट्टि तिरिगिति
वेतल-नेल्ल दीर्चि वर मोसगि

Madātmulaina durātma janulanu
Kathalanu pogaḍi pogaḍi
Sadā né varāla chuṭṭi tirigiti
Vetala nella dīrchi vara mosagi

सुमेरु-मध्य-निल्ये श्यामकृष्णुनि
सोदरी कौमारी
उमा मीनाक्षम्मा शङ्करी
ओ महाराज्ञी रक्षिञ्चुडु-किदिसमयमु

Suméru madhya nilayé śyāmakrishṇuni
Sódarī kaumārī
Umā mīnākshammā śankarī
O mahārājnī rakshinchudu kidisamayamu

Brahma, Vishnu and Siva eulogise your deeds!

You are the Ancient One! You are the Queen to whom Sarasvati and Indrani bow down!

You are the queen of the Lord, whom serpents adorn!

I have been wandering singing the praises of the proud and the wicked!

Remove my afflictions. Grant me your grace!

O! Goddess seated in the midst of Meru mountain! Sister of the darkhued Krishna! O! Eternal Maiden!

O! Uma! O! Mother Meenakshi! O! Sankari, Creatrix of good!

O! Great Queen! This is the time to save me!

राग : वराळि Rāga : Varāli

8. कामाक्षि बङ्गारुकामाक्षि ननु ब्रोववे
तामस मेल रावे सामगानलोले सुशीले

कामकालप्रिय भामिनी काम्य-
कामदे कल्याणी
कामाक्षी कञ्चदळायदाक्षी त्रि-
कोण वासिनी कारुण्यरूपिणी

Kāmākshi bangārukāmākshi nanu bróvavé
Tāmasa méla rāvé sāmagānalolé suśīlé

Kāmakāla priya bhāmini kāmya-
Kāmadé kalyānī
Kāmākshī kanchadaḷāyadākshī tri-
Koṇavāsinī kāruṇyarūpiṇī

पावनी मृदुभाषिणी भक्त-
पालिनी भवमोचनी
हेमाङ्गी हिमगिरिपुत्री म-
हेश्वरी ह्रींकाररूपिणी

Pāvanī mridu bhashiṇī bhakta-
Pālinī bhavamochanī
Hemāngī himagiri putrī ma-
Héśwarī hrinkārarūpiṇī

8. Kamakshi

O! Kamakshi, Love-eyed One! O! Golden Kamakshi! Protect me!

O! Good-natured One! Who is fond of Saama music, please come without delay!

O! Beloved of the Destroyer of Cupid! Granter of all that is desired! O! Auspicious One!

O! Kamakshi, Love-eyed One! Whose eyes are like lotus petals!

O! Dweller in the triangle! O! Embodiment of kindness!

O! Pure One! Who purifies! O! Softspoken One!

O! Protector of devotees! O! Goddess who grants liberation from Samsara!

O! Golden-limbed One! O! Daughter of the Snowy Mountain!

O! Great Goddess! Who manifests in the holy sound: Hrim!

श्याम कृष्ण परिपालिनी शुक
श्यामळे शिवशङ्करी
शूलिनी सदाशिव निकिराणि वि-
शालक्षतरुणी शाश्वतरूपिणी

नामनविविनु देवी नीवे गतियनि नम्मिनानु
मायम्मा वेगमे करुण जुडवम्मा बङ्गारुवोम्मा

Śyāma krishṇa paripālinī śuka
Śyāmalé śivaśankarī
Śūlinī sadāśivanikirāni vi-
Śālaksha tarunī śāśvata rūpiṇī

Nāmanavivinu devī nīvé gatiyani namminānu
Māyammā végamé karuṇa jūdavammā bangāru bommā

O! protector of Syamakrishna! O! dark One with the parrot! O! Auspicious Creatrix of good!

O! Tridentholder! Queen of the everauspicious Lord Siva!

Young Beloved of Siva, the wide-eyed One! One with everlasting manifestation!

O! Goddess! Listen to my thoughts!

I believe that you are my only refuge!

My Mother! Hurry and show me mercy! O! Golden Deity! Bangaru Bomma!

राग : कल्याणी Rāga : Kalyāni

9. बिरान वरालिञ्चि ब्रोवुमु निनुनेरनम्मिति

पुरारिमनो-हारिणी श्रीकामाक्षि

तामसमु-सेयकने नीवु करुणानिधि-गा
दा परामुखमिकनेल विनु सरोजमुखि

कामिताथ्र-फल-दायकी देवी नत-कल्प-लति-
का पुराणि मधुर-वाणि शिवुनिकिराणि

श्यामकृष्ण-सोदरि गौरी परमेश्वरी गिरि-
जा अनाथ रक्षणम्बु सलुपग-रावे

Birāna Varālinchi brovumu ninuneranammiti

Purārī mano hāriṇī Śrī Kāmākshi

Tāmasamu seyakané nīvu karuṇānidhi-gā
dā parāmukhmikanela vinu saroja mukhi

Kāmitartha phala dāyakī devī nata kalpa lati-
kā purāṇi madhura vāṇi śivunikirāṇi

Śyāmakrishṇa sodari gaurī paraméśwarī girijā anātha rakshaṇambu salupaga rāvé

9. Birana varalinchi

Speedily giving boons, protect me! I firmly believe in you!

You have stolen the heart of Siva, the Destroyer of Tripura! O! Auspicious Love-eyed One! Sri Kamakshi!

Do not delay! Are you not the treasurehouse of compassion? Why this indifference? Listen to me O! Lotusfaced One!

O! Goddess! Who grants whatever is desired! You are like the Kalpaka creeper (which fulfils all desires) to those who bow to you!

O! Ancient One! O! Sweetspoken One! O! Queen of the Auspicious Lord, Siva!

O! Sister of the darkhued Krishna! O! Fair One! O! Supreme Goddess! O! Daughter of the mountain Girija! You protect the orphaned. Please come!

राग : मध्यमावती | Rāga : Madhyamāvati

10. पालिंचु कामाक्षी पावनी पाप-शमनी अम्ब

चाला बहुविधमुगा निन्नु सदा वेडु-कोन्डि ना येन्देल
इलागु जेसेवु वेत हरिञ्चवे वेगमे नन्नु-

Pālinchu kāmākshi pāvanī pāpa śamani amba

Chālā bahu vidhamugā ninnu sadā veḍukonḍi nā yendela
Ilāgu jésévu veta harınchavé végamé nannu-

स्वान्तम्बुलोन निन्ने तलचे
सुजनुल-केल्ल-नेवेळ
सन्तोषमु-लोसगे-वनिनीवु
मनोरथ-फलदायिनिवनि
कान्तमगु-पेरुपोन्दितिवि (ई जगमु)
कारुण्य मूर्तिवै जगमु
कापाडिन तल्लिगदा नेनु
नीदु बिड्डनु लालिञ्चि

Swāntambulóna ninné talaché
Sujanula kella névéḷa
Santóshamu losagé vani nīvu
Manóratha phala dāyinivani
Kāntamagu péru ponditivi (ī jagamu)
Kāruṇya mūrtivai jagamu
Kāpāḍina talligadā nénu
Nīdu biḍḍanu lālinchi

10. Paalinchu Kamakshi

Protect me, O! Love-eyed One! Kamakshi! O! Purifier!

O! Destroyer of sins! O! Mother!

I have beseeched you in various ways!

Why treat me like this? Remove my sorrow and speedily protect me!

Good persons who think of you are bestowed happiness and since you are the granter of the fruits of desires

You have acquired the magnetic name: Embodiment of Kindness! Are you not the Mother who saved the universe?

I am your child! As my Mother, protect me!

ई मूर्ति यिन्त तेजो मयमै
यिटु-वले कीर्ति विस्पूर्ति
निट्लनु-गुणमूर्ति त्रिलोक
मुलो जूचिन यन्दैन-गलदा
एमो तोलिनोमु नोचितिनो
नी-पाद-पद्म-दर्शनमु
वेमारु लभिञ्चि कृतार्थुडनैति
नामनवि नालकिञ्चि

Ī mūrti yinta téjómayamai
Yiṭuvalé kīrti vispūrti
Nitlanu-gaṇamūrti triloka
Muló jūchina yandaina kaladā
Émó tolinómu nóchitinó
Nī pāda padma darśanamu
Vémāru labhinchi krutarthudanaiti
Nāma navi nālakinchi

This form of yours is radiant!
You are the embodiment of all virtues!

Can this glorious form of yours be seen anywhere else in the three worlds?

I have got this vision of your lotus feet several times due to some spiritual sadhana in previous births!

I feel blessed and gratified! Protect me, heeding my pleadings!

राजादि-राज-राजन्मकुटी-
तट-मणि-राज-पादा
ने जाल-निज-सन्निधिनि-कोरि
समस्त- जनुलकेल्ल वरदा
राजमुखी श्यामकृष्णनुता
काञ्ची पुरेश्वरी विकस-
राजीव-दळाक्षी जगत्साक्षी
यो-प्रसन्न-पराशक्ती

Rājādi rāja rājanmakuṭī
Taṭa maṇi rāja pādā
Né jāla nija sannidhini kóri
Samasta janula kella varadā
Rājamukhī śyāmakrishṇanutā
Kānchī puréśvarī vikasa
Rājīva daḷākshī jagatsākshī
Yó prasanna parāśaktī

कनक गिरि-सदन ललित निनु भजन
सन्ततमु चेयक जड्डनु
विनुमु निखिल-भुवन-जननिवि-इपुडु
मादुरितमु दीर्चि वरा-लिच्चि

Kanaka giri sadana lalita ninu bhajana
Santatamu chéyaka jaḍuḍanu
Vinumu nikhila bhuvana jaṇanivi-ipuḍu
Mā duritamu dīrchi varā lichchi

Your feet shine in the glow of gems set in the crowns of emperors who bow down to you!

I have often surrendered myself at your altar!

You bestow boons on all!

Your face is radiant! You are worshipped by Syamakrishna!

You are the Goddess of the city of Kanchi! Your eyes are like the fully bloomed lotus! You are the witness for the entire universe!

O! Supreme Power, ever gracious and pleased! Protect me!

O! Lalita, Playful Goddess! who reside in the golden mountain! I am a fool, not meditating on you constantly!

O! Mother of the entire universe! Listen!

Dispel my afflictions, grant me boons and protect me!

SONGS OF MUTHUSWAMI DIKSHITAR

(18th-19th Century A.D.)

	Song	*Rāga*
1.	Vatapi Ganapatim	Hamsadhwani
2.	Sri Moolaadhaara	Sri
3.	Subrahmanyena Rakshitoham	Suddhadhanyasi
4.	Meenakshi me mudam	Poorvikalyani
5.	Akhilandeswari	Dwijavanti
6.	Sree Venkatesagirisamaalokaye	Suruti
7.	Sree Ranga puravihara	Brindavana saranga
8.	Vallabha Nayakasya	Begada
9.	Akshaya Linga	Sankarabharanam
10.	Amba Neelayadakshi	Neelambari

MUTHUSWAMI DIKSHITAR

MUTHUSWAMI DIKSHITAR (1775-1835 A.D.)

Like Tyagaraja and Syama Sastri, Muthuswami Dikshitar, one of the Trinity of Carnatic Music, was born in Tiruvarur in the Thanjavur district of Tamil Nadu.

Inheriting music knowledge from his father, Muthuswami Dikshitar embellished it with his mastery of the Sanskrit language.

One special feature about the songs of Dikshitar is that they are all related to and centre around Deities in various temples in South India, to which he made pilgrimages throughout his life of sixty years.

Muthuswami Dikshitar composed his first song at the Subrahmanya temple at Tiruttani. He considered the Deity of this temple as his Guru and hence used the pen-name "Guru Guha" in all his musical compositions.

The major temples visited by Dikshitar and on whose deities he composed songs are: Tirupati, Kalahasti, Kancheepuram, Chidambaram, Madurai, Sri Rangam, Kumbhakonam, Tirunelveli, Rameswaram, Tiruchendur, Sabarimalai apart from Tiruvarur, his own hometown.

Though Bhakti or devotion is the main ingredient in his songs, this is tempered by Jnana or knowledge. One does not find the emotional exuberance of Tyagaraja or Syama Sastri in his songs.

Muthuswami Dikshitar was a Vedantin, in the tradition of Sankara, who believed in One Supreme Power and considered the deities worshipped as manifestations of that Supreme Power, who transcended name and form.

The songs of Dikshitar, composed in chaste Sanskrit and set to a variety of majestic tunes (both Carnatic and Hindustani), exude a feeling of serenity, dignity and bliss, characteristic of a truly evolved spiritual savant.

राग : हंसध्वनि Rāga : Hamsadhwani

1. वातापि गणपतिं भजेऽहं वारणास्यं वरप्रदं श्री

भूतादि संसेवित शरणं भूत भौतिक प्रपञ्चा भरणम्
वीतरागिणं विनतयोगिनं विश्वकारणं विघ्नवारणम्

पुराकुंभसंभव मुनिवरप्रपूजितं त्रिकोण मध्यगतम्
मुरारि प्रमुखाद्युपासितं मूलाधारक्षेत्रस्थितम्
परादिचत्वारिवागात्मकं प्रणवस्वरुपवक्रतुण्डम्
निरन्तरं निटिलचन्द्रखण्डं निजवामकर विधृतेक्षुदण्डम्
करांबुज पाश बीजापूरं कलुषविदूरं भूताकारम्
हरादि गुरुगुह तोषितबिंबं हंसध्वनिभूषित हेरंवम्

Vātāpi gaṇapatim bhajéham vārāṇasyam Varapradam śrī

Bhūtadi samsévita śaraṇam bhūta bhautika prapanchābharaṇam
Vītarāgiṇam vinatayoginam viśvakāraṇam vighnavāraṇam

Purā kumbha sambhava munivara prapūjitam trikoṇa madhyagatam
Murāri pramukhādyupāsitam mūlādhāra kshetra sthitam
Parādichatwāri vāgātmakam praṇavaswarūpavakra tuṇdam
Nirantaram niṭilachandra khaṇdam nija vāma kara vidhrute kṣhudaṇḍam
Karāmbuja pāśa bījāpūram kalushaviduram bhūtākāram
Harādi guruguha toshita bimbam hamsadhwani bhūshita hérambam

1. Vātāpi Ganapatim

I worship Vatapi Ganapati,* who is elephant faced, grants boons and is ever auspicious!

I worship Him, whose feet are worshipped by the Elemental Powers, who bears the five elements of earth, water, air, fire and ether and the worlds created out of them,

Who is without passion, to whom the Yogis bow down, the cause of the universe, the Remover of obstacles.

I worship Vatapi Ganapati, who was in ancient past worshipped by the great sage, Agastya, who is seated in the centre of the triangular yantra,

Who is meditated upon by Vishnu and other prominent persons, who is situated in the Mooladhara cakra,

Who exists in the four modes of speech: *Para, Pasyanti, Madhyama* and *Vaikhari*, Whose form is the Pranava sound: AUM, Who has a curving trunk, Who always has the crescent moon on the forehead, Who holds the sugarcane stump in His left hand, Who has in His lotus hands the rope, pomegranate fruit, guava etc, the sinless One, Who has gigantic form, Whose form pleases Siva, Subrahmanya and others, Who is pleased by the raga, Hamsadhwani, the Elephantfaced One!

*Vatapi Ganapati is the Deity in Tiruvarur, the hometown of Dikshitar.

राग : श्री Rāga : Śrī

2. श्री मूलाधार चक्रविनायक अमूल्यवरप्रदायक

मूलाज्ञान शोक विनाशक मूलकन्द मुक्तिप्रदायक

सकळिकृत देवादि देव शबळीकृत सर्वज्ञस्वभाव
प्रकटीकृत वैखरीस्वभाव पराभव प्रसिद्धगजग्रीव
विकट षट् शत श्वासाधिकार विचित्राकार भक्तोपकार
अकळङ्क विभास्वर विघ्नेश्वर हर गुरु गुह सोदर लंबोधर

Śrī mūlādhāra chakravināyaka amūlyavarapradāyaka

Mūlagnāna śokavināśaka mūla kanda mukti pradāyaka

Sakaḷikrita devādideva śabaḷīkrita sarvajna swabhāva
Prakaṭīkrita vaikharī swabhāva parābhava prasiddha gajagriva
Vikaṭa saṭśata śwāsādhikāra vichitrākāra bhaktópakāra
Akaḷanka vibhāswara vighnéśwara hara guru guha sódara lambódhara

2. Sri Moolaadhaara

O! Vinayaka, who have no leader above you! seated in the Moolaadhaara cakra! Granter of invaluable boons!

You destroy the sorrow arising from basic ignorance! You are the root of all existence! You are the One who grants liberation!

You are the primordial God of all gods! Who knows everything (all variegations of knowledge)!

Your nature is to make manifest the mode of speech known as Vaikhari!

You are peerless! You are the famous elephantfaced One!

You are Vikata, the Huge One! You rule over the six hundred breaths! Your form is peculiar and unique! You help your devotees!

You shine stainlessly like the sun! You lord over obstacles! You are the Destroyer! You are the brother of Subrahmanya! You have the big stomach!

O! Vinayaka seated in the Moolaadhaara cakra!

राग : शुद्धधन्यासी Rāga : Suddhadhanyāsi

3. सुब्रह्मण्येन रक्षितोऽहं अष्टादश लोचनखण्डेन

प्रब्रवामादि पूजितपदेन पुरन्दर मनोल्लासकरणेन

कङ्कशैल विहारेण वरेण वल्ली देवसेना रमणेन
अकारवृत्तेन सानन्देन भोग मोक्षदानेन नित्येन
वेङ्कटेश्वर सुपूजिन विचित्र विशाख महोत्सवेन
शुकरहस्य प्रकाशगुरुगुहेन कृत्तिकासुत शुद्ध धन्येन

Subrahmanyena rakshitóham ashtādaśa lóchanākhaṇḍéna

Prabravāmādi pūjitapadéna purandara manóllāsa karaṇéna

Kankaśaila vihārēṇa vareṇa vallidévasénā ramaṇéna
Akāravritténa sānandéna bhóga mókshadānéna nityéna
Vénkatéśwara supūjiténa vichitra viśākha mahótsavéna
Śukarahasya prakāśa guru guhéna krittikasuta śuddha dhanyéna

3. Subrahmanyéna rakshitoham

I am protected by Subrahmanya, who shines in a universal form with eighteen eyes!

His feet are worshipped with mantras like Prabravama! He is the One who has made Indra happy!

He resides in the Kanaka hills, He is the venerable One! He is the Lord of Valli and Devasena!

He shines as the first letter of the alphabet! He is ever blissful! He grants enjoyment and liberation! He is the Eternal One!

He is well worshipped by King Venkatesvara! He has a great festival in the month of Vaisakha! He revealed the secret of Sage Suka! He is Guruguha, the Teacher! He is the son of Goddess Krittika! He has a pure reputation!

I am protected by Subrahmanya!

राग : पूर्वीकल्याणी Rāga : Poorvikalyāni

4. मीनाक्षिमेमुदं देहि मेचकाङ्गि राजमातङ्गि

मानमातृमेये माये मरकतछाये शिवजाये मीनलोचनि

पाशमोचनि मानिनि कदंबवनवासिनि

मधुरापुरिनिलये मणिवलये मलय ध्वज पाण्ड्य राजतनये
विधु विडंबन वदने विजये वीणागान दशगमकक्रिये
मधुमदमोदित हृदये सदये महादेव सुन्दरेशप्रिये
मधुमुररिपुसोदरि शातोदरि विधि गुरुगुह वशंकरि शंकरि

Meenākshi mé mudam déhi méchakāngi rājamātangi

Mānamātruméyé māyé marakatachhāyé śivajāyé mīnalochani
Pāśamochani mānini kadambavanavāsini

Madhurā puri nilayé maṇi valayé malaya dhwaja pāṇḍya rājatanayé
Vidhu viḍambana vadané vijayé vīṇāgāna daśagamakakriyé
Madhumada modita hrudayé sadayé mahādéva sundaréśa-priyé
Madhu muraripu sódari sātódari vidhi guruguha vaśankari śankari

4. Meenaakshi me mudam

O! Meenakshi! Goddess with fishlike eyes! Whose form is of emerald! O! Daughter of King Matanga! Give me bliss!

You exist as the knowable and the unknowable and as the knowledge to measure these!

You shine with the green emerald splendour! You are the spouse of Siva! Your eyes resemble fish!

You grant liberation from earthly bondage! You reside in the Kadamba forest!

Your temple is in the city of Madurai! You wear gemset bangles! You are the daughter of King Pandya whose flag carries the Malaya emblem!

Your face shames the moon! You create ten gamakas in the music of your lute!

Your heart delights in tasting honey! You are compassionate! You are the Beloved of the Great God Sundaresa!

You are the sister of Vishnu who is the enemy of the demons Madhu and Mura! You are slim waisted! You are the Creatrix of good who captivate Brahma and Subrahmanya!

O! Meenakshi! Give me bliss!

राग : द्विजावन्ति Rāga : Dwijāvanti

5. अखिलाण्डेश्वरि रक्ष मां आगम संप्रदाय निपुणे श्री

निखिललोक नित्यात्मिके विमले निर्मले श्यामळे सकल कले

लंबोदर गुरुगुह पूजिते लंबालकोद्भासिते हासिते
वाग्देवताराधिते वरशैलराजनुते शारदे

जंभारि संभाविते जनार्दननुते जुजावन्तिरागनुते
जल्ली मद्दळ झर्झर वाद्य नाद मुदिते ज्ञानप्रदे

Akhilāṇḍéśwari raksha mām āgama sampradāya nipuṇé śrī

Nikhila loka nityātmiké vimalé nirmalé śyāmaḷé sakala kalé

Lambodara guru guha pūjité lambālakodbhāsité hasité
Vāgdévatārādhité varaśaila rājanuté śāradé
Jambhāri sambhāvité janārdananuté jujāvanti rāganuté
Jallī maddaḷa jharjhara vādya nāda mudité gnānapradé

5: Akhilandeswari

O! Ruler of the entire manifest universe! Protect me!

O! Auspicious One who can be realised through scriptural sadhana!

You are the immortal soul in all creation!

O! Stainless One! O! Pure One! O! Darkhued One! Embodiment of all arts!

O! Goddess worshipped by Ganesa and Subrahmanya! You look beautiful due to the hair loops falling on your forehead! O! Smiling One!

You are worshipped by Sarasvati, the Goddess of speech!

You are worshipped by the great Mountain King! O! Sarada!

You are venerated by Indra! worshipped by Vishnu! praised through the raga Jujavanti!

You rejoice in the sound of various drums like jalli, maddala and jarjara! O! Granter of knowledge!

O! Ruler of the entire manifest universe! Protect me!

राग : सुरुटि Rāga : Suruṭi

6. श्रीवेङ्कटेश गिरीशमालोकये विनायक तुरगारूढम्

देवेशपूजित भगवन्तं दिनकर कोटि प्रकाशवन्तं गोविन्दम्
नत भूसुर वृन्दं गुरुगुहानन्दं मुकुन्दम्

अलमेलुमङ्गा समेतं अनन्तपद्मनाभमतीतम्,
कलियुग प्रत्यक्ष विभातं कञ्जजादिदेवोपेतम्
जलधरसन्निभ सुन्दरगात्रं जलरुह मित्राब्ज शत्रुनेत्रम्
कलुषापह गोकर्णक्षेत्रं करुणारसपात्रं चिन्मात्रम्

Śrī Venkateśa girīśamālókayé vināyaka turagārūdham

Dévéśa pujita bhagavantam dinakara koṭi prakāśavantam góvindam
Nata bhūsura brindam guru guhānandam mukundam

Alamélu manga samétam anantapadmanābhamatītam
Kaliyuga pratyaksha vibhātam kanja jādidévópétam
Jaladhara sannibha sundara gātram jalaruha mitrābja śatru nétram
Kalushāpaha gokarṇa kshétram karuṇārasa pātram chinmātram

6. Sree Venkatesagirisamaalokaye

Let us look at the Lord of Venkata Hills, who rides on Garuda, the King of birds!

Let us look at:

the Radiant Lord, worshipped by Indra, Lord of angels, who shines with the radiance of a million suns, who is Govinda, who herds cows (and words)

One who is worshipped by hordes of angels, Mukunda, the granter of liberation who gives happiness to Guruguha (Subrahmanya)!

Let us look at:

the Lord, who is accompanied by Alamelumanga (Sri Lakshmi), the endless Lord with lotus in the navel, the One who is beyond everything,

Who shines as the manifest God in the Kali age, who is with Brahma and other angels,

Whose body is beautiful like the dark rainladen cloud, whose eyes are the sun and the moon,

Who is located in the Gokarna temple which destroys sins,

Who is the citadel of mercy, who exists as consciousness.

राग : बृन्दावन सारंग — Rāga : Brindāvana sāranga

7. रंगपुरविहार जयकोदण्ड रामावतार रघुवीर श्री

अंगज जनक देव बृन्दावनसारंगेन्द्र वरद रमान्तरंग
श्यामळांग विहंग तुरंग सदयापांग सत्संग

पङ्कजाप्तकुल जलनिधि सोमवर पङ्कजमुख पट्टाभिराम
पदपङ्कजजितकाम रघुराम
वामाङ्क गत सीतावरवेषशेषाङ्क शयन भक्त सन्तोष
येणाङ्कर विनयन मृदुतर भाष
अकळङ्क दर्पण कपोल विशेषमुनि संकटहरण गोविन्द वेंकटरमण मुकुन्द
संकर्षण मूल कन्द शंकर गुरुगुहानन्द

Ranga puravihāra jayakodaṇda rāmāvatāra raghuvīra śrī

Angaja janaka déva brindavana sārangéndra varada
ramāntaranga
Śyāmaḷānga vihanga turanga sadayā pānga satsanga

Pankajāptakula jala nidhisómavara pankajamukha
paṭṭābhirāma pada pankaja jitakāma raghurāma
Vamānka gata sītā vara vésha śéshānka śayana bhakta santosha
yenānkara vinayana mridutara bhāsha
Akaḷanka darpaṇa kapóla viśésha munisankataharaṇa govinda
vénkata ramaṇa mukunda
Sankarshaṇa mūla kanda śankara guruguhānanda

7. Rangapuravihara

Hail! O! Resident of the city of Srirangam! O! Scion of the Raghu family who incarnated as Rama!

You are the father of Cupid, the god of love! Who protected groups of angels and granted boons to the elephant king! Who resides in the heart of Lakshmi!

You have a darkhued body! Whose vehicle is the King of birds, Garuda! Whose glance is ever compassionate! You exist wherever the righteous are.

You are the moon to the sea which is the Surya clan! Your face is like the lotus! You are Rama who enjoyed the coronation!

Your feet are like lotuses! You have overcome desires!

You are Raghurama!

You have Sita on your left lap! You lie on Adi Sesha, the serpent king! You make your devotees happy!

Your eyes are the sun and the moon! You are softspoken!

Your cheeks resemble stainless mirrors! You remove the sorrows of sages! You are Govinda!

You are Venkata Ramana! You are Mukunda! Sankarshana!* You are the root of all beings! You give happiness to Sankara and Subrahmanya!

Hail! O! Resident of Sriranga city!

*Lit. = one who holds together, an epithet of Balarama, one of the ten incarnations of Vishnu.

राग : बेगड Rāga : Bégaḍa

8. वल्लभानायकस्य भक्तो भवामि वाञ्छितार्थ दायकस्य
वरमूषिक वाहनस्य

पल्लवपद मृदुतरस्य पाशाङ्कुशादि धरस्य
मल्लिका जाती चंपक हारस्य मणिमालस्य
वल्ली विवाह कारणस्य गुरूगुह पूजितस्य
काळीकला मालिनी कमलाक्षि सन्नुतस्य

Vallabha nāyakasya bhaktó bhavami vāncchitārtha dāyakasya
Vara mūshika vāhanasya

Pallava pada mrudu tarasya pāśānkuśādi dharasya
Mallikā jātī champaka hārasya maṇimālasya
Vallī vivāha kārṇasya guru guha pūjitasya
Kāḷīkalā mālinī kamalākshi sannutasya

8. Vallabha Nayakasya

I am the devotee of the Lord of Vallabha, who gives whatever is desired!

And whose vehicle is the great mouse!

I am the devotee of:

the One whose feet are soft like tender shoots! Who holds the rope and the axe!

Who wears the garland of jasmine and champak flowers as also of gems!

Who was the cause of Valli's marriage! Who is worshipped by Subrahmanya!

Who is venerated by Kaali, Sarasvati and the lotuseyed Lakshmi!

राग : शंकराभरणम् Rāga : Sankarābharaṇam

9. अक्षयलिंग विभो स्वयंभो अखिलाण्डकोटिप्रभो पाहि शंभो

अक्षरस्वरूप अमित प्रताप आरूढ वृषवाह जगन्मोह
दक्ष शिक्षण दक्षतरसुर लक्षणविधि विलक्षण लक्ष्य
लक्षण बहु विचक्षण सुधा भक्षणगुरू कटाक्ष वीक्षण

पदरीवन मूल नायिका सहित भद्रकाळीश भक्त विहित
मदन जनकादिदेव महित माया कायै कलना रहित
सदय गुरूगुह तात गुणातीत साधु जनोपेतशंकर नवनीत
हृदय विभात तुंबुरू संगीत हींकार संभूत हेमगिरिनाथ
सदाश्रित कल्पक महीरूह पदांबुज भवरथ गज तुरग पदाति संयुत
चैत्रोत्सव सदाशिव सच्चिनान्द मय

Akshayalinga vibhó swayaambhó akhilaandakóṭi parbhó
pāhi śambhó

Aksharaswarūpa amitapratāpa ārūḍha vrushavāha jaganmoha
Daksha śikshaṇa daksha tarasura lakshaṇavidhi vilakshana
lakshya
Lakshaṇa bahu vichakshaṇa sudhā bhakshaṇa guru kaṭāksha
vīkshaṇa

Padarīvana mūla nāyikā sahita bhadrakāḷiśa bhakta vihita
Madana janakādi déva mahitā māyā kārya kalanārahita
Sadaya guruguha tāta guṇātīta sādhujanópéta śamkara navanīta
Hradaya vibhāta tumburu sangīta hrīnkāra sambhūta
hemagirinātha
Sadāśrita kalpaka mahīruha padāmbuja bhavaratha gaja turaga
padāti samyuta
Chaitrotsava sadāśiva sachchidānanda maya

9. Akshayalinga

O! Lord whose form is decayless! O! Lord who are born out of yourself! You are the Lord of all beings! Protect me, O! Originator of good!

Your form is immortal! Your fame is infinite! You are seated on your vehicle, the bull! You captivate the whole universe with your beauty!

You were clever in punishing Daksha! You are the protector of the angels! You are superior to Brahma, the creator!

You are skilled in arts and literature! You drink nectar!

The glance of your eyes is great and powerful!

O! Lord who stays in the forest of *jujupe* trees with the primordial heroine! O! Lord of Bhadrakali! Who is bound by devotees!

Venerated by Vishnu and other gods! Who have no interest in illusory deeds!

Father of the compassionate Subrahmanya! Who is beyond attributes! Attainable by good persons! Doer of good!

You shine with a heart that melts like butter! Who is born out of the sound *Hrim* produced by the musical instrument Tumburu! Lord of the golden Mountain!

You are like the wishfulfilling creeper, Kalpaka, to those who seek refuge in you! Whose feet are like lotuses! O! Creator! In whose Chaitra festival you have the fourfold army of chariots, elephants, horses and infantry! O! ever Auspicious One! Who exist as existence, consciousness and bliss!

राग : नीलांबरि Rāga : Neelāmbari

10. अंबा नीलायताक्षि करुणाकटाक्षि अखिल लोक साक्षिकटाक्षि

बिबांधरि चित्प्रतिबिंबाधरि बिन्दुनादवशंकरि शंकरि
अंबुजा रमण सोदरि अतिरथि अंबरि कादंबरि नीलांबरि

शिवराज धानि क्षेत्र वासिनी श्रितजन विश्वासिनि
शिव कायारोहणे शोल्लासिनि चिद्रूप विलासिनि

नव योगिनि चक्रविकासिनि नवरस दर हासिनि
स्वर्णमय विग्रह प्रकाशिनि स्वर्णमय हासिनि
भुवनोदय स्थितिलय विनोदिनि भुवनेश्वरि क्षिप्रप्रसादिनि
नवमाणिक्य वल्लकी वादिनि भव गुरूगुह वेदिनि संमोदिनि

Ambā nīlayadākshi karuṇā katākshi akhila loka sākshi katākshi

Bimbādhari chitpratibimbādhari bindunāda vaśankari śankari
Ambujāramaṇa sódari atirathi ambari kādambari nilāmbari

Śivarājadhāni kshetra vāsini śritajana viśwāsini
Śivakāyāróhaṇé śollāsini chidrūpa vilasini

Navayogini chakra vikāsini navarasa dara hāsini
Swarṇamaya vigraha prakāśini swarnamaya hāsini
Bhuvanodaya sthitilaya vinodini bhuvaneśwari kshipraprasādini
Navamāṇikya vallakī vādini bhava guruguha védini sammodini

10. Amba neelaayadaakshi

O! Mother! Whose eyes are like blue lilies! Whose glance exudes compassion! O! Witness to all the worlds! Cast your glance on me!

Your lips are red like the Bimba fruit! Who is reflected in consciousness! Who is captivated by Bindu and nada! O! Creatrix of good!

You are the sister of Vishnu, the Lord of Lakshmi! You fight fiercely from the chariot! You shine with the saffron flower! O! Kaadambari! You wear the blue garment!

You live in the royal household of Lord Siva! Who does not let down those who seek refuge in you!

You sport in ascending the body of Siva! You shine as Pure Consciousness!

You shine in the Srichakra comprising the nine Yoginis!

You smile exuding the nine emotions!

You shine with a golden form! You laugh while speaking beautiful words!

You delight yourself in sport while creating, maintaining and destroying the universe! You are the Queen of the universe! You are easily pleased!

You play the lute studded with nine types of gems! You are known by Siva and Subrahmanya! You are ever blissful!

O! Mother! cast your glance on me!

SONGS OF SWATI TIRUNAL

(19th Century A.D.)

	Song	*Rāga*
1.	Maamava sadaa	Kaanadaa
2.	Visvesvar	Sindhubhairavi
3.	Paripalaya	Rītigowla
4.	Saarasasamamukha	Khamaas
5.	Bhavayaami Raghuraamam	Raagamaalikaa
6.	Smarajanaka	Behaag
7.	Smara Haripaadaaravindam	Saama
8.	Deva deva kalayaami te	Maayaamaalavagowla
9.	Pankajalochana	Kalyaani
10.	Raasa vilaasa	Kaamboji

SWATI TIRUNAL

SWATI TIRUNAL (16 April 1813-25 December 1846 A.D.)

Maharaja Swati Tirunal lived only for a short period of 33 years but has bequeathed to us a veritable treasure of nearly 400 God-oriented songs, mostly in Sanskrit.

Swati Tirunal used to say: "All that I write, whether poetry or music, centres round God. This is an act of faith with me. Music is not worth its name otherwise."

Swati Tirunal was a contemporary of the Carnatic musical Trinity: Tyagaraja, Muthuswami Dikshitar and Syama Sastri but did not meet any of them.

Ascending the throne at the age of sixteen, Swati Tirunal ruled over the state of Travancore for nearly 18 years till his death. He was an enlightened ruler and a patron of poets, artists and performers. Music was in his bloodstream and many musicians flocked to his royal court. Interaction with the dance masters and dance troupes from Thanjavur inspired Swati Tirunal to compose several forms of music for dance like Tillanas, Varnas, Padas and Svarajatis. Swati Tirunal also imbibed the best from the many Hindustani musicians who flocked to his court and composed many songs in Hindustani ragas.

He was devoted to Lord Padmanabha, the deity in the Tiruvanathapuram temple, but he saw no distinction between Siva and Vishnu, whom he considered as two forms of the same Divinity. His famous song *Visvesvar darsan* exemplifies this philosophy of his.

Very few rulers could come anywhere near Swati Tirunal in his patronage of arts, his catholicity of religious outlook, his transcendence of narrow regional, religious and caste barriers. He was a truly evolved royal sage.

राग : कानडा

Rāga : Kānadā

1. मामव सदा जननि महिषासुर सूदनि

सोमबिंब मनोहर सुमुखी सेवकाखिल
काम दान निरत कटाक्षविलासिनि

Māmava sadā janani mahishāsura sūdani

Sómabimba manóhara sumukhi sévakākhila
Kāma dāna nirata katāksha vilāsini

पुरविमतवदन पङ्केरुह मधुपे!
नारदमुख मुनुमौनि निकर गेय चरिते!
सरसीरुहासनादि सुरसमुदयमणि
चारुमौळिविराजित चरणांबुज युगले!

Puravimata vadana pankéruha madhupé!
Nārada mukha munu mowni nikara géya charīté!
Sarasīruhāsanādi surasamudayamaṇi
Chārumowḷi virājita charaṇāmbuja yugaḷé!

1. Maamava sadaa

O! Mother! Destroyer of the demon Mahisha! Ever protect me!

You have a beautiful, sweet face, which resembles the moon!

You are ever engaged in granting the desires of all your devotees, with the flash of your glance!

You are the bee which drinks the honey in the lotus flower which is the face of Siva, the Destroyer of Tripura!

Your legends are sung by multitudes of sages headed by Narada!

Your pair of lotus feet shine with the beautiful jewelled heads of the celestial community headed by the lotus-seated Brahma!

कनक भासुर दिव्य कला पराजित गात्रि!
वनरुहादळातोपविभञ्जन रुचि नेत्री!
मुनिगण संमोहन माननीय मृदुहासे!
विनतजन कल्पकवल्लरी! गिरिसुते!

Kanaka bhasura divyakala parajita gātri!
Vanaruha dala topa vibhanjana ruchi nétri!
Munigana sammóhana mananıya mriduhāsé!
Vinatajana kalpaka valları! Girisute!

कुरु मे कुशलं सदा कमलनाभानुजे!
निरवति भव खेदनि वारण निरते!
चारुनूतन घन सदृशराजित वेणि!
दारुण दनुजाळिदारण पटु चरिते!

Kuru me kusalam sada kamalanabhanuje!
Niravati bhava khédanivaraṇa nirate!
Charunutana ghana sadrusa rajita veṇi!
Daruṇa danujaḷi dāraṇa patu charite!

O! daughter of the mountain!

Your body outrivals the radiance of gold!

Your eyes destroy the pride of the lotus petals!

Your venerable gentle smile captivated the sages!

You are the Kalpaka creeper to the people who bow to you!

Ever bestow me prosperity, O! Sister of Vishnu, who has the lotus in the navel!

You are ever engaged in removing the many sorrows of the phenomenal world!

Your hair is like the beautiful new cloud!

You have a history of being competent in destroying the array of ruthless demons!

Ever protect me, O! Mother! Slayer of Demon Mahisha!

राग : सिन्धुभैरवि Rāga : Sindhubhairavi

2. विश्वेश्वर दर्शन कर चल मन तुम कासी

विश्वेश्वर दर्शन जब किनहो बहु प्रेम सहित
काटे करुणा निधान जनन-मरण फान्सी

बहती जिनकी पुरी मो गंगा पय के समान
वाके तट घाट घाट भर रहे सन्यासी

भस्म अंग भुज त्रिशूल उर मे लसे नागमाल
गिरिजा अरधंग धरे त्रिभुवन जिन दासी

पद्मनाभ कमलनयन त्रिनयन शंभुमहेश
भज ले इन दो स्वरूप रहिये अविनासी

Viśvéśvar darśan kar chal man tum kāsī

Viśvéśvar darśan jab kinho bahu prém sahit
Kāṭé karuṇā nidhān janan-maraṇ phānsī

Bahtī jinkī purī mo gangā paya ké samān
Vāké taṭ ghāṭ ghāṭ bhar rahé sanyāsī

Bhasm ang bhuj triśūl ur mé lasé nāgmāl
Girijā ardhang dharé tribhuvan jin dāsī

Padmanābh kamalnayan trinayan Śambhu Mahéś
Bhaj lé in do swarūp rahiyé avināsī

2. Visvesvar darsan

O! Mind! Go to Kasi and see Visvesvar!

When someone has darshan of Lord Visvesvar with deep love,

The Lord, who is the treasurehouse of mercy, cuts the hangrope of birth and death.

In His city, the river Ganga flows like milk and the river banks and all the ghats are filled with sanyasis.

His limbs are covered with ashes, He has the trident in His hands, on His chest a garland of snakes,

He holds Girija as half of His body, all the three worlds serve Him.

He is the lotus-eyed Padmanabha as also the three-eyed Siva, the Great Lord, the Creator of bliss!

Worship both these forms and attain immortality.

राग : रीतिगौळ Rāga : Rītigowla

3. परिपालय मां श्रीपद्मनाभ मुरारे

शरणागतत भरणोत्सुक शारदसोम समानन
विरिञ्च सुरेश्वर सेव्य

तामरसायत लोचन चारुतनो धरणीधर वन
दामविराजित दारुणदनुभव घन विपिनदहन

दानमतङ्गज चारुविलासगते तपनीयवसन मुनि-
मानसतामरसालय मणिमय मकुट परिलसित

नीलघनोपम सुन्दरदेहरुचे निखिलामर भयहर
शैलसुताधवसन्नुत शमय मम सकल गदमिह

Paripālaya mām śrīpadmanābha murāré

Śaraṇāgatata bharaṇótsuka śārada sóma samānana
Virinchi suréśvara sevya

Tāmarasāyata lochana chārutanó dharaṇīdhara vana
Dāma virājita dāruṇadanubhava ghana vipinadahana

Dāna matangaja chāruvilāsa gaté tapanīyavasana muni
Mānasa tāmarasālaya maṇimaya makuta parilasita

Nīlaghanópama sundara déharuché nikhilāmara bhayahara
Śailasutā dhavasannuta śamaya mama sakala gadamiha

3. Paripalaya maam

Protect me, O! Sri Padmanabha! Enemy of demon Mura!

O! Lord! Whose face is like the autumnal moon! You are eager to accept those who seek refuge in you!

You are served by Brahma and Indra!

Your eyes are like the red lotus, O! Lord with the beautiful body!

You held the earth, O! Wearer of the garland of wild lotuses!

You burn the dense forests which are the ruthless demons!

Your step is beautiful like that of the wild elephant!

You wear golden ornaments!

You reside in the lotus hearts of sages. You shine with the bejewelled Crown!

You have a beautiful body which resembles the blue clouds!

You destroy the fears of all the celestial angels.

O! Lord worshipped by the spouse of the daughter of the mountain!

Cure all my afflictions here!

राग : खमाज़ Rāga : Khamās

4. सारससममुख परमव मां
सनकमुखविनुत (सारस)

पाररहितभव घोर कलुषतर-
वारिराशि परिपतितमयि सदय (सारस)

Sārasasamamukha paramava mam
Sanaka mukha vinuta (Sārasa)

Pārarahita bhavaghóra kalushatara-
Vārirāśi paripatitamayi sadaya (Sārasa)

कुटिल भुजगवरफणकृत सुरुचिरनटन देव
गोकुल कलशपयोनिधि पूर्णशशांक
निटिल तटलसित मृगमद तिलक सु
नीलवारिदशरीर यदुतिलक (सारस)

Kuṭila bhujagavara phaṇa kruta suruchiranaṭana deva
Gokula kalaśa payó nidhi pūrṇa śaśānka
Niṭila taṭa lasita mruga mada tilaka su
Nīla vārida śarīra yadutilaka (Sārasa)

4. Sārasa samamukha

O! Lord, whose face is equal to the lotus, you are worshipped by Sanaka and other sages! Protect me!

O! Compassionate One! Protect me, who has fallen into this sea of samsara, which has no shore beyond, is terrifying, and full of sorrow.

O! Lord, who danced on the hood of the wicked serpent, Kaaliya, you are the moon which rose out of the milky ocean of Gokula!

You wear the musk mark on the forehead, you are darkhued like the blue clouds, and the Scion of the Yadava clan. Protect me!

मदनजनक नवमणिमयसुललितहार शौरे
मञ्जुलवचन विमोहित विबुधनिकाय
पदनतनिखिल मनोरथदायक
पापजाल गिरिकुलिश सरसतर (सारस)

Madanajanaka navamaṇimaya sulalita hāra śauré
Manjula vachana vimóhita vibudhanikāya
Padanata nikhila manórathadāyaka
Pāpa jāla giri kuliśa sarasatara (Sārasa)

सकलभुवन भयहरण पटुचरितजालामेय
सन्ततं विहर मे मनसीह दयालो
प्रकटबलदनुज भेदनलोलुप
पद्मनाभ भुजगाधिपतिशयन (सारस)

Sakala bhuvana bhaya haraṇa paṭucharita jālāméya
Santatam vihara mé manasīha dayālό
Prakaṭa bala danuja bhédanalólupa
Padmanābha bhujagādhipati śayana (Sārasa)

O! Lord! Father of the god of love! who wear garlands set with the nine gems, Born in the lineage of Sura, who captivated the hordes of angels with your sweet speech, who grant all the desires of those who fall at your feet, who are the thunderbolt to the mountain of accumulated sin heaps, the Supreme Enjoyer! Protect me!

O! Padmanabha! Lord with the lotus in your navel! You have a history of being competent in destroying the fears of all the worlds! Your fame is measureless! You are the Compassionate One! You have destroyed powerful demons! You lie on Adi Sesha, the serpent King! Relax in my heart!

रागमालिका — Rāgamālikā

सावेरी — Sāverī

5. भावयामि रघुरामं भव्य सुगुणारामम्
भावुकवितरणपरापाङ्ग लीला लसितम्

Bhāvayāmi raghurāmam bhavya suguṇarāmam
Bhāvukavi taraṇa parāpānga līlā lasitam

नाट्टकुरिञ्जि — Nāṭṭakurinji

दिनकरान्वयतिलकं दिव्यगाधिसुतसवना-
वनरचितसुबाहुमुखवधमहल्यापावनम्
अनघमीश शापभङ्गं जनकसुताप्राणेशम्
घनकुपितभृगुरामगर्वहरमितसाकेतम्

Dina karānvayatilakam divyagādhisuta savanā
Vanarachita subāhu mukha vadhamahalyā pāvanam
Anaghamīśa śāpa bhangam janaka suta prāṇēśam
Ghanakupita bhrugurāma garva hara mita sāketam

धन्यासि — Dhanyāsi

विहिताभिषेकमथा विपिनगतमार्यवाचा
सहित सीता सौमित्रिं शान्ततमशीलम्
गुहनिलयगतं चित्रकूटागतभरतदत्त
महित रत्नमय पादुकं मदन सुन्दराङ्गम्

Vihitābhishékamatha vipina gata mārya vāchā
Sahita sītā soumitrim śāntatamaśīlam
Guha nilaya gatam chitrakūṭāgata bharata datta
Mahitaratnamaya pādukam madana sundarāngam

5. Bhavayami Raghuramam

I meditate on Raghu Rama, the garden of good qualities like humility

The one who shines with the sport of distributing welfare to all with his glance!

I meditate on:

the Chief of the solar race, who accompanied Viswamitra to the forest

And killed demons like Subahu and purified Ahalya,

Broke the great bow of Siva and became the husband of Sita, the daughter of Janaka,

Destroyed the pride of Parasurama, who was very angry, and returned to Ayodhya.

I meditate on:

Raghu Rama, who went to the forest, losing his coronation, to keep his father's word,

accompanied by Sita and Lakshmana, the son of Sumitra,

Whose conduct was marked by supreme patience!

Who went to the house of Guha,

And gave Bharata, who came to Chitrakoota, the pair of sandals studded with valuable jewels,

Rama, whose limbs are as beautiful as those of the god of love.

मोहनम् Mohanam

विततदण्डकारण्य गत विराधदळनम्

सुचरितघटजदत्तानुपमितवैष्णवास्त्रम्

पतगवरजटायुनुतं पञ्चवटीविहितावासम्

अतिघोरशूर्प्पणखावचनागत खरादिहरम्

Vitatadaṇḍakāraṇya gata virādhadaḷanam
Sucharita ghaṭa dattānu pamita vaishṇavāstaram
Pataga varajaṭāyu nutam panchavaṭi vihitāvāsam
Atighora śūrppaṇakhā vachanagata kharādiharam

मुखारि Mukhāri

कनकमृगरुपधरखलमारीचहरमिह सु-

जनविमत-दशास्य हतजनकजान्वेषणम्

अनघं पम्पातीरसङ्गताञ्जनेय-नभोमणि-

तनुज सख्यकरं वालितनुदलनमीशम्

Kankamrugarūpa padhara khalamārīcha haramiha su
Janavimata daśāsya hruta janaka jānveshaṇam
Anagham pampātīra samgatānjanéyanabhomaṇi
Tanuja sakhyakaram vālitanudalanamīśam

I meditate on Raghu Rama

Who went through the extensive Dandakaranya forest and killed the demon Viradha,

and got the inimitable Vaishnava arrow from Sage Agastya of good character,

Who was worshipped by the Chief of birds, Jatayu and stayed for a while in Panchavati

and destroyed demons like Khara who came to fight, incited by the terrible demoness, Soorpanakha!

I meditate on Raghu Rama

Who slew the evil Maareecha, who assumed the form of the golden deer

and searching for Sita, the daughter of Janaka, stolen by the ten-headed Ravana, the enemy of the people

came to the bank of the pure Pampa river and with the help of Hanuman, the son of Anjani, made friends with Sugriva, the son of Sun,

and split the body of Vali,

the Lord who is replete with riches!

पूर्वीकल्याणी Poorvikalyāni

वानरोत्तमसहित वायुसूनुकरार्पित-
भानुशत भास्वर भव्यरत्नाङ्गुलीयम्
तेन पुनरानीतान्यून चूडामणिदर्शनम्
श्रीनिधिमुदधितीरेश्रितविभीषण मिलितम्

Vānarottamasahita vāyusunukarārpita
Bhānu śata bhāswara bhavyaratnāngulīyam
Tena punarānītā nyūna chūḍāmaṇi darśanam
Śrīnidhi mudadhitīré śrita vibhīṣaṇa militam

मध्यमावती Madhyamāvati

कलितवर सेतुबन्धं खल निस्सीम पिशिताशन-
दलन मुरु दशकण्ठ विदारणमतिधीरं
ज्वलनपूतजनक सुतासहितं यात साकेतं
विलसित पट्टाभिषेकं विश्वपालं पद्मनाभं

Kalitavara sétubandham khala nissīma piśitāśana
Dalanamuru daśa kanṭha vidāranamatidhīram
Jwalanapūta janaka sutā sahitam yāta sākétam
Vilasita paṭṭābhishékam viśwapālam padmanābham

I meditate on Raghu Rama

who, while with the great monkey Sugriva, gave his ring set with nine gems and shining like a hundred suns into the hands of Hanuman, the son of Wind and saw it again when brought back by Hanuman (after showing it to Sita)

and on the seashore met Vibhishana who sought refuge in the Lord, on whom sits Lakshmi, the goddess of prosperity.

I meditate on Raghu Rama

who made competently the Sethu bridge in the ocean, destroyed several demons and killed Ravana who had ten necks,

and returned to Ayodhya, accompanied by Sita, the daughter of Janaka, purified by fire,

and had the coronation with pomp and splendour,

the Protector of the universe, who exists as Lord Padmanabha, the Lord with the lotus in the navel!

राग : बेहाग् Rāga : Behāg

6. स्मरजनक शुभचरिताखिल लोकनायक मामव (स्मर)

ततरुणासारस दळनयन तपणीयरुचिवसनधर
तनुविनिन्दित नीरद दूत नारदाहतभरिद (स्मर)

पापदहण सुरविमत पाटनप्रसित
श्रीपते जलनिधिशयन भवतापन शन पटुतर (स्मर)
पावनसुगुण निरुपम भानुशशिनयन
देवदेव पुरारि कमलजदिविषदधिपति वन्दित (स्मर)
पालित भुवन समुदय परमपुरुषहरे
फालशोभित सुरभि मृगुमद पद्मनाभ जगन्नुत (स्मर)

Smara janaka śubhacharitākhila loka nāyaka māmava (Smara)

Tataruṇāsārasa daḷanayana tapaṇīya ruchivasanadhara
Tanuvinindita nīradadruta nāradāhata bharida (Smara)

Pāpadahaṇa suravimata pāṭana prasita
Śrīpaté jalanidhi śayana bhavatāpana śana paṭutara (Smara)
Pāvana suguṇa nirupama bhānuśaśi nayana
Déva déva purāri kamala jadi viṣadadhipati vandita (Smara)
Pālita bhuvana samudaya parama purusha Haré
Phāla śóbhita surabhi mrugumada Padmanābha jagannuta (Smara)

6. Smarajanaka

O! Father of the god of love! O! Lord with an auspicious character! O! master of the three worlds! Protect me!

Your eyes are like the petals of the red lotus!

You wear the golden garment!

Your body rivals the cloud. You accept the prostrations of Narada offered profusely.

You destroy sins. You are renowned in chasing away the enemies of angels!

O! Lord of Lakshmi! Who lies on the ocean! You are an expert in putting out the fiery afflictions of this world.

You have pure good qualities! You are peerless!

The sun and the moon are your eyes!

O! God of gods! You are worshipped by Siva, Brahma and Indra!

You protect the welfare of the world! O! Supreme Person! O! Hari!

Your forehead shines with sweetsmelling musk! O! Padmanabha! To whom the universe bows! Protect me!

राग : साम Rāga : Sāma

7. स्मर हरिपादारविन्दं मुदानिशम् (स्मर)

तरसा जहि ममतां दारसुतादिषु
कुरु सज्जनसंगममुरु पुण्यसमवाप्यम् (स्मर)

Smara haripādāravindam mudāniśam (Smara)

Tarasā jahi mamatām dārasutādishu
Kuru sajjanasangamamuru puṇya samavāpyam (Smara)

यदिह लभसे बत वित्तं तेन
मुदमवाप्नुहि भाग्यायत्तम्
उदयं संसेव्य धनमदिरामत्तं हन्त
मा खेदय चित्तमहो मुधा (स्मर)

Yadiha labhasé bata vittam téna
Mudamavāpnuhi bhāgyāyattam
Udayam samsévya dhana madiramattam hanta
Mā khedaya chittamaho mudhā (Smara)

7. Smara Hari paadaaravindam

Remember always the lotus feet of Vishnu!

Give up quickly the possessive attachment to wife and children!

Cultivate the company of good people, which is possible only due to accumulated virtue!

Be happy with the wealth which you get here in this world due to your good fortune!

Do not pain your heart by serving someone who is drunk with the wine of wealth and is unkind!

हरिमन्दिरे वस नित्यं
काममयि मा मा वद बतासत्यं
परमिह भज सदा माधव भृत्यं
पावनतरनिजकृत्यमहो मुदा (स्मर)

Harimandiré vasa nityam
Kāmamayi mā mā vada batāsatyam
Paramiha bhaja sadā mādhava bhrityam
Pāvana tara nija krityamaho mudā (Smara)

परमपुरुषमनुवारं भज
पद्मनाभमलमुदारं
करुणापूर्णनयनमसितशुभशरीरं
कलित कौस्तुभनवहारमहो मुदा (स्मर)

Paramapurushamanuvāram bhaja
Padmanābha malamudāram
Karuṇāpūrṇa nayana masitaśubhaśarīram
Kalita kaustubha navahāramaho mudā (Smara)

Stay always in the temple of Hari, Vishnu!

Never ever speak untruth.

Serve always the devotee of God who performs pure deeds.

Blissfully worship always the Supreme Person, Padmanabha, the Pure One, the generous One, whose eyes exude compassion, has a beautiful darkhued body,

and wears the garland of Kaustubha gem!

राग : मायामाळवगौळ

Rāga : Māyāmāḷavagowḷa

8. देव देव कलयामि ते चरणांबुज सेवनं
भुवनत्रय नायक भूरिकरुणया मम
भवतापमखिलं वारय रमाकान्त

Deva deva kalayāmi té charaṇāmbuja sévanam
Bhuvana traya nāyaka bhūrikaruṇayā mama
Bhava tāpamakhilam vāraya ramākānta

परम हंसाळिगेय पवित्रतर घोर
दुरित हर चरित दिन मनुश्रवण निरत
परिजन निकर कामितार्थ परिपूरणलोलुप
भूरि मनोज्ञ पाङ्ग

Parama hamsāḷigéya pavitratara ghóra
Durita hara charita dina-manuśravaṇa nirata
Parijana nikara kāmitārtha paripūraṇa lolupa
Bhūri manogna pānga

8. Deva Deva kalayami te

O! Lord! O! God! I shall worship your lotus feet!

O! Lord of the three worlds! O! Beloved of Lakshmi! with total compassion towards me, ward off all my sorrows of this world!

O! Purest of the Pure! You are sung by Paramahamsas (Evolved sages)!

O! Lord! You are eager to hear daily the stories about the removal of afflictions of your devotees!

You are ever interested in fulfilling the desires of multitudes of devotees with your glance, competent in the knowledge of what their minds desire!

वारण दुस्सहार्ति वारण बहुनिपुण
पुरुहूतामर पूजित भव्यचरणयुग
विरचय शुभमयि विशदनाभिजात
भारतीश कृतनुतिपरमदुष्ट भगवन्

Vāraṇa dussahārti vāraṇa bahunipuṇa
Puruhūtāmara pūjita bhavya charaṇayuga
Virachaya śubha mayi viśada nābhijāta
Bhāratīśa krutanutiparama dushṭa bhagawan

जातरूपनिभचेल जन्मार्जितं ममाखिल
पातक सञ्चयमिह वारय करुणया
दितिजालि विदळन दीनबन्धो मामवा
श्रितविबुधासाल श्रीपद्मनाभ शौरे

Jātarūpanibhachéla janmārjitam mamākhila
Pātaka sanchayamiha vāraya karuṇayā
Ditijāli vidaḷana dīnabandhó māmavā
Śrita vibudhāsāla śrī padmanābha śauré

O! Lord who very competently removed the hardship of the elephant!

Whose pair of venerable feet is worshipped by celestials like Indra!

Do good to me, O! Radiant Lord! Who is worshipped by Brahma, the Lord of Saraswati, who is born out of your pure navel!

O! Lord! who wear the golden garment!

Kindly remove the whole burden of sin accumulated over several births!

O! Lord who destroyed the hordes of demons!

O! Friend of the afflicted! Protect me!

You are a protective support for the angels who seek refuge in you! O! Sri Padmanabha! O! Sauri!*

*Descendant of Sura.

राग : कल्याणी

Rāga : Kalyāni

9. पङ्कज लोचन पाहि मुरान्तक
पङ्कजालयाजीवनाथ विभो (पङ्क)

शंकर विधि वलशासननुतगुण
शंकुरुसत्तं मे सारसनाभ शौरे (पङ्क)

Pankaja lóchana pāhi murāntaka
Pankajālayā jīvanātha vibhó (Panka)

Śankara vidhi vala śāsananutaguṇa
Śankuru sattam mé sārasanābha śouré (Panka)

त्रिभुवन घातुकं दितिजं कनककशिपुमभि
भूयनखरै र्विदीर्य बलाद्रभसेन निज
पाद राजीव नतमेतत्प्रभावम्
श्रीनरसिम्ह प्रह्लादं पालितवान् (पङ्क)

Tribhuvana ghātukam ditijam kanakakaśipu mabhi
Bhūyan kharair vidīrya balādrabhasena nija
Pāda rājīva natametat prabhāvam
Śrī narasimha prahlādam pālitavān (Panka)

9. Pankaja lochana

O! Lotuseyed One! O! Destroyer of demon Mura! Protect me!

O! Lifelord of Lakshmi who resides in the lotus! O! Lord!

Siva, Brahma and Indra bow before your qualities!

Do me good always O! Lord with the lotus in the navel! O! Sauri!

Violently overwhelming the demon Hiranyakasipu, the afflictor of the three worlds and splitting him open with your claws O! Narasimha! Man Lion! You protected Prahlada!

Please protect me!

पितृवचसा समुत्पेत्य बिपिनभुव
मतिरूपगुणामात्मधर्मपत्नीम्
हृतवन्तं दशकण्ठमिषुणैकेन निहत्य
प्रतिगृह्यैनां साकेतं प्राप्त श्रीरघुवीर (पङ्क)

Pitru vachasā samutpétya vipina bhuva
Matirūpaguṇā mātma dharma patnīm
Hrutavantam daśakanṭhamishuṇaikéna nihatya
Pratigrihyainām sāketam prāpta śrī raghuvīra (Panka)

सुन्दर तररूपनन्दिता भीरनारी
वृन्दमुख सरसीरुहमधुप
बृन्दावनान्त कृत विविध सुख विहार
कुन्दनिभरदगोविन्द नन्द नन्दन (पङ्क)

Sundara tararūpananditā bhīranārī
Vrundamukha sarasīruha madhupa
Brundāvanānta kruta vividha sukha vihāra
Kunda nibharada govinda nanda nandana (Panka)

Keeping up your father's word, you went to the forest and killing with arrows the ten-necked Ravana, who stole your wife of great beauty and qualities, you returned to Ayodhya, O! Rama, Scion of Raghus!

Please protect me!

With your beautiful form you pleased hordes of Gopi women, as the bee does the lotus!

and indulged in pleasurable sport in Brindavan O! Govinda! Son of Nanda! whose teeth rival the jasmine flowers!

Please protect me!

राग : काम्बोजी Rāga : Kamboji

10. रासविलासलोलो लसति भवान् देव (रास)

भासुरकाळिन्दीपरिसरे मधुवने (रास)

केशभारनिबद्धकेकिबर्हो निकामम्
पेश लमणि भूष पीतवसनशाली
नाशयन्निह कुसुमाशुगमदं कान्त्या
केशवो मृदुविहसवदनो मुनिगेयकीर्ति
रमलमूर्तिरतिपावनो जगति (रास)

Rāsavilāsalóló lasati bhavān déva (Rāsa)

Bhāsura kāḷindī parisaré madhuvané (Rāsa)

Keśa bhāra nibaddha kékibarho nikāmam
Pésa lamaṇi bhūsha pītavasana śālī
Nāśayanniha kusumāśugamadam kāntyā
Keśavo mridu vihasa vadano munigéya kīrti
Ramalamūrti rati pāvano jagati (Rāsa)

10. Raasavilaasa

O! Lord! You shine as one interested in the sport of love!

In the sweet forest in the vicinity of the Kaalindi river you shine as one interested in the sport of love!

You wear the peacock feather in your crest of hair!

You wear beautiful gemset ornaments!

You wear the yellow garment!

With your magnetic body you destroy the arrogance of Cupid, the god of love!

You have a smiling face!

Your fame is eulogised by sages!

Your body is flawless and you are pure at heart!

You shine in this world as Krishna, the slayer of the demon Kesi.

मदनातुरगोपिका मण्डलमध्यगतो
मुदमनुपमं तासां मुरळीरवेण दिशन्
तदतुलगानमुदितलोल मौलिरिह
पदयुग विलसन्नवमणिनूपुरभव्यनाद
विजितहंसनिनदो रमारमण (रास)

Madanā turagópikā maṇḍala madhyagató
Mudamanupamam tāsām muraḷīravéṇa diśan
Tadatulagānamudita lola mouliriha
Padayugavilasannava maṇi nūpura bhavyanāda
Vijita hamsaninadó ramā ramaṇa (Rāsa)

विविधनर्मालापनवीटीदानचुम्बन-
प्रवितत भुजा श्लेषादि विलासशतैरहो
विवशयन्नमुं यदुवीर गोपीसञ्चयम्
दिवि समुपागतनिर्जरसन्नुत दिव्यशोभ
जलजनाभ शरणागताधिहर (रास)

Vividhanarmālāpana vīṭīdānachumbana-
Pravitata bhujāśleshādi vilāsaśatairahó
Vivaśayannamum yaduvīra gopīsanchayam
Divisamupāgata nirjarasannuta divyaśobha
Jalajanābha śaraṇāgatādhihara (Rāsa)

You are in the midst of lovelorn cowherdesses,

You give them excessive happiness with your flute music!

Listening to the songs of the Gopis, you nod your head in joy!

The gemset anklets on your feet produce an auspicious sound, which outrivals the song of swans!

O! Lord of Lakshmi! You are in a mood to engage in the sport of love!

You have captivated the hordes of Gopis (cowherdesses) with your sweet speech, *paan*-giving, kissing and embracing with your extended arms, etc.

You are eulogised by the angels who have lined up in heaven!

O! Resplendent One! O! Padmanabha! Who destroy the sorrows of those who seek refuge in you!

You seem inclined to engage in the sport of love!

SONGS OF RABINDRANATH TAGORE

(19th-20th Century A.D.)

	Song	*Rāga*
1.	Jeevan jakhan sukaai jaay	Jayajayanti
2.	Aamaar khelaa jakhan cchilo	Mishra Malhar
3.	Roopasaagare doob diyecchi	Khamas
4.	Tumi keman kore gaan	Behag
5.	Jagate aananda yajne aamaar nimantran	Sarfarda
6.	Taayi tomaar aanando	Mishra Jayajayanti
7.	Aaji sravanaghanagahan	Mishra Gaud Malhar
8.	Aami hethai thaaki	Vasanta
9.	Aamaare tumi ashesh kareccho	Malhar
10.	Ekati namaskaare	Paras

RABINDRANATH TAGORE

RABINDRANATH TAGORE (7 May 1861-7 August 1941 A.D.)

Rabindranath Tagore, the first Indian to get the Nobel Prize for Literature, though a multifaceted creative genius was basically a mystic-philosopher-poet, who saw the universe with all its colour and beauty as the joyful expression and manifestation of God.

His songs are imbued with this message and soaked in the culture, tradition and philosophy of India.

The songs of Rabindranath Tagore included in this book are his God-oriented outpourings contained in his famous *Gitanjali*, which won him the Nobel Prize.

The songs of Tagore in original Bengali, sung all over Bengal in sweet melodious tones, are termed *Rabindra Sangeet* and are part of the psyche of the people of Bengal.

The same intensity of God-intoxication seen in other mystic saints who lived centuries earlier and were devoted to personified manifestations of God is seen in the songs of Tagore, though he did not limit his devotion and adoration to a particular form or Deity.

For him, God was omnipresent as the Supreme Power. Nor was he otherworldly. "Deliverance is not for me in renunciation. I feel the embrace of freedom in a thousand bonds of delight" was his message.

It is this approach—and the beauty of the Bengali language—that invests his songs with such captivating charm.

राग : जयजयन्ती

Rāga : Jayajayantī

1. जीवन जखन शुकाए जाय करुणाधाराय एसो,
सकल माधुरी लुकाए जाय गीतसुधारसे एसो॥
कर्मजखन प्रबल आकार गरजि उठिया ढाके चारि धार
हृदय प्रान्ते, हे जीवननाथ, शान्त चरणे एसो।।
आपनारे जबे करिया कृपण कोणे पड़े थाके दीन हीन मन
दुआर खुलिया, हे उदार नाथ, राजसमारोहे एसो॥
वासना जखन बिपुल धुलाय अंध करिया अबोधे भुलाय,
ओहे पवित्र, ओहे अनिद्र, रुद्र आलोके एसो॥

Jīvan jakhan śukāyé jāi karuṇādhārāy yéso,
Sakala mādhurī lukāyé jāi gītasudhārase yéso//
Karma jakhan prabal ākār garji uṭhiyā dhake chāri dhār
Hrudayaprānté, hé jīvan nāth, śānt charaṇé yéso//
Āpnāré jabé kariyā krupaṇ koṇé paḍé thāké dīn hīn man
Duār khuliyā, hé udār nāth, rāj samārohé yéso//
Vāsanā jakhan vipul dhulāi andh kariyā abodhé bhulāy,
Óhé pavitr, ohé anidr, rudr āloké yéso//

1. Jeevan jakhan sukaai jaay

When life becomes dried up, come with a shower of compassion.

When all sweetness is lost, come with the nectar of songs.

When work, assuming powerful form, creates deafening noise on all sides, O! Lord of my life! Step into my heart with your peacebearing feet.

When my mind lies locked up in a corner, poor and needy, O! Generous Lord! Come with royal splendour!

When sensory weakness becomes overpowering and blinds and deludes me, O! Pure One! O! Ever Wakeful One! Come like the Destroyer with thunder and light!

राग : मिश्र मल्हार — Rāga : Mishra Malhār

2. आमार खेला जखन छिलो तोमार सने
तखन के तुमि ता के जानतो,
तखन छिलो ना भय, छिलो ना लाज मने, जीवन बेहे जेतो अशान्तो॥
तुमि भोरेर बेला डाक दिएछो कतो
जेनो आमार आपन सखार मतो,
हेंसे तोमार साथे फिरे छिलाम छुटे से दिन कतो-ना बन-बनान्तो॥
ओगो, सेदिन तुमि गाइते जे सब गान
कोनो अर्थो ताहार के जानतो
शुधु संगे तारि गाईतो आमार प्राण, सदा नाचतो हृदय अशान्तो॥
हठात् खेलार शेषे आज की देखि छोबि,
स्तब्धो आकाश, नीरब शशि रोबि,
तोमार चरणपाने नयन कोरि नतो भुबन दाँडिए आछे एकान्तो॥

Āmār khelā jakhan cchilo tomār sané
Takhan ke tumi tā ke jānto
Takhan cchilo nā bhay, cchilo nā lāj mane, jīvan béhé jéto aśānto//
Tumi bhorer belā dāk diyeccho kato
Jénó āmār āpan sakhār mato
Hénsé tomār sāthé phirécchilām cchuṭé sé din kato nā ban banānto//
Ogo sédin tumi gāyite je sab gān
Kono ārtho tāhār ke jānto
Śudhu sange tāri gāyito āmār prāṇ sadā nachto hrudai aśānto//
Haṭhāt khélār śeshé āj, kī dekhi cchobi,
Stabdho ākāś, nīrab śaśi robi,
Tomār charaṇ pāné nayan kori nato bhulan dāḍiye ācché yékānto//

2. Aamaar khelaa jakhan cchilo

When my play was with you, I did not know who you were.

Then there was no fear or modesty in the mind. Life was restless.

At dawn you would wake me up from sleep like a friend.

In your company I used to roam all day in the forests.

Those days what songs you sang to me, I never knew their meaning.

Only my life sang the same tunes and my restless mind always danced.

Suddenly, after the play is over, what do I see?

The still sky, the silent moon and stars and the whole world lies in loneliness to see your feet.

राग : खमाज़ | Rāga : Khamās

3. रूपसागरे डुब दियेछि अरुपरतन आशा करि,
घाटे घाटे घुरबो ना आर भासिए आमार जीर्ण तोरी॥
समय जेन हयरे एबार ढेउ खावया सब चुकिए देवार
सुधाय एबार तलिए गिए अमर होये रबो मोरी।।
जे गान काने जाय ना सोना से गान जेथाय नित्य बाजे
प्राणेर बीणा निए जाबो सेई अतलेर सभा माझे।।
चिरदिनेर सुरटि बेंधे शेष गाने तार कान्ना केंदे
नीरव जिनि ताँहार पाए नीरब बीणा दिबो धरि।।

Rūp sāgaré dub diyécchi arūpratan āśā kari
Ghāte ghate ghurbo nā ār bhāsiye āmār jīrṇ tórī//
Samay jen haire yebār dheu khāvaya sab chukiye devār
Sudhāi yebār taliye giye amar hoye rabo móri//
Je gān kāné jāi nā sonā se gān jethāi nitya bāje
Prāṇer bīṇā niye jābo seyi atler sabhā mājhé//
Chirdiner suraṭi béndhé śesh gané tār kānnakéndé
Nīrab jini tāhār pāye nīrab bīṇa dibó dhari//

3. Roopasāgaré doob diyecchi

Desiring to obtain the pearl of the formless, I dive into the sea of forms.

I will no longer sail from ghat to ghat in my weather-beaten boat.

The days when I enjoyed being tossed by the waves are over.

Now I want to merge with the Immortal.

I want to take this lute of my life to that bottomless assembly where those songs ever sound, which are silent and do not reach the ears. I shall tune my lute to the notes of the Immortal and after finishing the rest of my songs, lay it down at the feet of the Ever Silent One.

राग : बेहाग

Rāga : Behāg

4. तुमि केमन कोरे गान करो हे गुणी,
आमि अबाक् होए शुनि, केवल शुनि ॥
सुरेर आलो भुवन फेले छेये,
सुरेर हावया चले गगन बेये,
पाषाण टुटे व्याकुल बेगे धेये
बहिया जाय सुरेर सुरधूनी ॥
मोने कोरि ओमनि सुरे गाई,
कंटे आमार सुर खुंजे ना पाई,
कोइते की चाइ, कोइते कथा बाँधे-
हार मेने जे परान आमार काँदे
आमाय तुमि फेलेछ कोन फाँदे
चौदिके मोर सुरेर जाल बुनि ॥

Tumi kéman koré gān karó hé guṇī/
Āmi abāk hoye śuni kéval śuni//
Surér ālo bhuvan phélé cchéyé
Surer hāvayā chalé gagan béyé
Pāshāṇ ṭuṭe vyākul bégé dhéyé
Bahiyā jāi surer surdhūnī//
Mone kori omani sure gāyī
Kanṭé aamaar sur khunjé nā paayee
Koite ki chāyi, koite kathā bandhe
Hār méné jé parān āmār kānde
Āmār tumi phelecch kon phānde
Chaudike mor surér jāl buni//

4. Tumi keman kore gaan

I do not know how you sing, O! Good Lord!
I just listen in silent wonder.
Your Divine radiance lights up the cosmos!
Your Divine breath of life moves as wind in the sky!
Breaking all barriers, the stream of your Divine music flows.
I wish to join you in singing, but my throat cannot find a voice.
I want to speak, but my speech is stifled.
You have made me a captive in the magical mesh of your divine music!

राग : सरफरदा Rāga : Sarfardā

5. जगते आनन्दयज्ञे आमार निमन्त्रण।
धन्य होलो, धन्य होलो मानबजीबन।
नयन आमार रुपेर पुरे, साध मिटोए बेडाय घुरे,
श्रवण आमार गभीर सुरे होएछे मगन।
तोमार जोज्ञे दिएछो भार, बाजाइ आमि बाँसी-
गाने गाने गेथे बेड़ाइ प्राणेर कान्ना हासि।
एखन समय होएछे कि? सभाय गिए तोमाय देखि,
जयध्वनि सुनिए जाबो, ए मोर निबेदन॥

Jagte ānandyajne āmār nimantraṇ/
Dhanya hóló, dhanya hóló mānabjīban/
Nayan āmār rūpré puré sādh miṭóyé bedāi ghuré,
Śravaṇ āmar gabhīr suré hóyecché magan/
Tómār jogné diyeccho bhār, bājāyi āmi bānsī-
Gāné gāné géthé bédāyi prāner kānnā hāsī/
Yékhan samay hoyeccheki? sabhāi giyé tomāy dékhi,
Jayadhwani suniye jābo yé mór nibédan//

5. Jagate ananda yajne aamaar timantran

This invitation to the joyous festival of the universe makes me feel blessed, my life blessed.

My eyes have seen and enjoyed all the sights in this city of forms.

My ears have heard all that needs to be heard.

You have given me my turn and I have played my flute and singing song after song, my life has ended.

Has the time come now to go behind the stage, see you and offer my thanks?, I ask.

6. राग : मिश्र जयजयंती Rāga : Mishra Jayajayantī

ताई तोमार आनन्दो आमार पर, तुमि ताई एसेछो नीचे।
आमार नोइले त्रिभुबनेश्वर, तोमार प्रेम होतो जे मीछे।
आमाय निए मेलेछो एई मेला
आमार हियाय चलछे रसेर खेला,
मोर जीबने बिचित्ररूप धोरे तोमार इच्छा तरंगिछे।
ताई तो तुमि राजार राजा होए
तबु आमार हृदय लागि
फिरछो कतो मनोहरण बेशे प्रभु, नित्य आछो जागि।
ताई तो प्रभु जेथाय एलो नेमे
तोमारि प्रेम भक्तप्राणेर प्रेमे।
मूर्ति तोमार जुगल सम्मिलने सेथाय पूर्ण प्रकाशिछे॥

Tāyī tomār ānando āmār par, tumi tāyī yeseccho nīché/
Āmār noyile tribhuvanéśvar tomār prem hótó jé mīché/
Āmāy niyé meleccho yéyī mélā
Āmār hiyāi chalacche rasér khéla,
Mor jībane bichitrarup ghóré tómār icchā tarangicche/
Tāī to tumi rajār rājā hóyé
Tabu āmār hruday lāgi
Phirccho kató manóharan beśe prabhu, nitya āccho jāgi/
Tāyī to prabha jethāi yeló némé
Tomāri prém bhaktprāṇer prémé
Mūrti tómār jugal sammilné sethāi pūrṇ prakāśicche//

6. Taayi tomaar aanando

You have come down to me, because your joy in me is full.

O! Lord of the three worlds! If I did not exist where would your love be?

You have taken me as a partner in all this festive fair.

The play of your delight moves in my heart.

Your wishes have taken myriad shapes in my life.

For this, You, King of kings, have adorned yourself and remained awake to captivate my heart. That is why O! Lord! Your love merges in the love of your devotees.

Your form fully shines in the perfect union of the devotee and you.

राग : मिश्र गौड़ मल्हार Rāga : Mishra Gaud Malhār

7. आजि श्रावणघनगहन मोहे गोपन तबो चरण फेले
निशार मतो नीरब ओहे, सबार दिठि एड़ाए एले।
प्रभात आजि मुदेछे आँखि, बातास बृथा जेतेछे डाकि,
निलाज नील आकाश ढाकि निबिड़ मेघ के दिलो मेले।
कूजनहीन कानन भूमि, दुआर देवया सकल घरे-
एकेला कोन पोथिक तुमि पथिकहीन पथेर परे।
हे एका सखा, हे प्रियतम, रोएछे खोला ए घर मम-
समुख दिए स्वपन सम जेओ ना मोरे हेलाय ठेले॥

Āji śrāvaṇaghanagahan mohe gópan tabo charan phélé
Nisār mato nīrab óhé sabār dithi yéḍāyé yélé/
Prabhat āji mudecche ānkhi, bātās bruthā jetecche ḍāki
Nilāj nīl akās ḍhāki nibid mégh ké diló mélé/
Kūjanahīn kananabhūmi du ār devayā sakal gharé-
Yékéla kón póthik tumi pathikahīn pathér paré/
Hé yékā sakhā hé priyatam, royecché khóla yé ghar mama-
Sumukh diyé svapan sam jéo nā móré hé lāi ṭhele//

7. Aaji Sravanaghanagahan

Today, in the darkness of the rainladen clouds of *Sravana*, You roam around silently.

Quiet as the night and eluding the eyes of all.

Today, the morning has closed its eyes, despite the beseechings of the east wind.

In the blue sky, the thick curtain of clouds has been drawn.

The forests are without the chirpings (of birds), the doors are shut in every home.

You are the only traveller in the deserted paths.

O! my only friend! my dearest Beloved! The doors are open in my home. Please do not pass by me like a dream!

राग : वसन्त Rāga : Vasanta

8. आमि हेथाय थाकि शुधु गाइते तोमार गान,
दिओ तोमार जगत-सभाय एइटुकु मोर स्थान।
आमि तोमार भुबन माझे, लागि नि, नाथ, कोनो काजे-
शुधु केवल सुरे बाजे अकाजेर एइ प्राण।
निशाय नीरब देवालए तोमार आराधन,
तखन मोरे आदेश कोरो गाइते हे राजन।
भोरे जखन आकाश जुड़े बाजबे बीणा सोनार सुरे,
आमि जेन ना रोइ दूरे एइ दियो मोर मान॥

Āmi hethāi thāki śudhu gāyité tomār gān,
Dió tomār jagat-sabhāi yeituku mór sthān/
Āmi tomār bhuvan mājhé lagini, nāth kónó kājé-
Śudhu keval suré bājé akājér eyi prāṇ/
Niśāi nīrab devālayé tomār ārādhan,
Takhan moré ādéś kóró gāyité hé rājan/
Bhóré jakhan ākāś juḍé bājbé bīṇā sonār suré,
Āmi jen nā royi dūré yeyi diyó mór mān//

8. Aami hethai thaaki

I am here only to sing your songs.

In this assembly of the world you have given me only a corner seat.

O! Lord! In this world of yours I am not engaged in any useful work.

This workless life can merely play meaningless tunes.

When it is time for worship at the temple in the silent night,

O! King! order me to sing.

When the golden lute sounds in the morning air,

Order me to be present and honour me.

9. राग : मल्हार Rāga : Malhār

आमारे तुमि अशेष करेछो, एमनि लीला नबो।
फुराए फेले आबार भरेछो, जीवन नव नव॥
कतो जे गिरि कतो जे नदी-तीरे
बेडाले बहि छोटो ए वाँसीटिरे,
कतो जे गान बाजाले फिरे-फिरे
काहारे ताहा कबो॥
तोमारि आई अमृतपरशे आमार हियाखानि
हारालो सीमा बिपुल हरषे, उथलि उठे बाणी॥
आमार शुधु एकटि मुठि भरि
दितेछ दान दिवस-विभावरी-
हलो ना सारा कतो ना जुग धरि
केवलि आमि लबो॥

Āmāre tumi aśesh karecchó yemani līlā nabó
Phurāyé phélé abar bharecchó jivan nav nav//
Kató jé giri kató jé nadī-tīré
Bedāle bahi cchoto ye bānsitire,
Kató jé gān bājālé phiré-phiré
Kāhāre tāhā kabó//
Tomāri āyī amrut parśé āmār hiya khāni
Hārālo sīmā bipul harshe uthli uṭhe bāṇī//
Āmār sudhu yekati muṭhi bhari
Ditecch dān divas-vibhāvari
Haló na sārā kató na jugdhari
Kévali āmi labó//

9. Aamaare tumi ashesh kareccho

You have made me immortal. This is your sport.

You empty this vessel time and again and ever fill it with new life.

How many times you have carried this small bamboo flute over hills and river banks!

Again and again how many songs you have sung through it!

At your immortal touch, my little heart loses its limits in great joy and bursts forth in words.

These small hands of mine are filled with fabulous gifts by you.

How many eons pass, and still you continue to bestow your gifts. And I remain to receive!

10. राग : परज़ Rāga : Paras

एकटि नमस्कारे; प्रभु, एकटि नमस्कारे
सकल देह लुटिए पड्डुक तोमार ए संसारे॥
घन श्रावण मेघेर मत, रसेर भारे नम्र नत
एकटि नमस्कारे, प्रभु, एकटि नमस्कारे
समस्त मन पड़िया थाक तब भवनद्वारे॥
नाना सुरेर आकुल धारा, मिलिए दिए आत्मद्वारा
एकटि नमस्कारे, प्रभु, एकटि नमस्कारे
समस्त गान समाप्त होक नीरब पाराबारे।
हस जेमन मानसयात्री
तेमनि सारा दिवसरात्रि
एकटि नमस्कारे, प्रभु, एकटि नमस्कारे
समस्त प्राण उड़े चलुक महामरण पारे॥

Yékaṭi namaskāre; prabhu, yékati namakāré
Sakal deh lutiyé paduk tómar ye samsāré//
Ghan śrāvaṇ méghér mat rasér bharé namra nat
Yekaṭi namaskāré prabhu, yekaṭi namaskārē
Samast man paḍiyā thāk tab bhavan dwāré//
Nānā surér ākul dhārā miliye diye atmadwārā
Yekaṭi namaskāré prabhu yékéti namaskāré
Samast gān samāpt hok nīrab pārābāré/
Has jéman mānasayātrī
Temani sāra divasrātri
Yékaṭi namaskāré, prabhu, yékaṭi namaskāré
Samast prāṇ ude chaluk mahāmaraṇ pāré//

10. Ekati namaskaare

In one prostration, O! Lord! in one prostration to you,
Let my whole body enjoy this world which lies at your feet.

Like the heavy rainladen cloud of *Sravana*, bending with the burden of unshed showers,
In one prostration, O! Lord! in one prostration to you,
Let my whole mind lie at your doorstep.

Let the diverse strains of my songs mingle and merge into one stream and flow to the sea of silence.
In one prostration to you, O! Lord! in one prostration to you!

Like the flock of homesick swans flying back to their mountain nests day and night,
In one prostration to you, O! Lord! in one prostration to you,
Let all of my life travel to its eternal home, beyond death!

SONGS OF SUBRAMANIA BHARATI

(19th-20th Century A.D.)

	Song	*Rāga*
1.	Ettanaikodi inbam vaittai iraiva	Bhoopalam
2.	Karpaga Vinayaka	Nata
3.	Villinaiyotta	Sindhu Bhairavi
4.	Muruga Muruga	Nattakurinji
5.	Vellai Tamarai	Bhimpalas
6.	Varuvai Varuvai Kanna	Poorna Chandrika
7.	Kaakkai Siraginile Nandalala	Kalyana Vasantam
8.	Kaayile Pulippadenne	Mand Bahar
9.	Teeratavilayaattu Pillai	Ragamalika
10.	Ninnai Saranadainthen	Punnagavarali

SUBRAMANIA BHARATI

SUBRAMANIA BHARATI (11 December 1882-12 September 1921 A.D.)

Subramania Bharati, the doyen of Tamil poets, was a philosopher, besides being an ardent patriot of the pre-Independence era in India. Though he lived only a short life of 39 years, his poetic output was prodigious.

Subramania Bharati was a deeply religious person, though he did not believe in orthodoxy and rigidities of caste distinctions.

He believed in the brotherhood of mankind and considered God as the Supreme Power manifesting as and guiding the universe. Though he was an *advaitin* at heart, he also believed in the various manifestations of Divinity as Krishna, Muruga, Ganesa, Devi or Shakti etc.

His devotional songs are a veritable granary of devotion and spirituality.

Bharati's approach to God has similarities with that of Rabindranath Tagore. Like the latter, he also saw the universe with all its colour and beauty as the joyful expression and manifestation of God. The first of the 10 songs selected for this volume bears this out.

But unlike Tagore, Bharati, in the tradition of the earlier mystic saints, was also devoted to personal manifestations of God.

Of the devotional songs included in this volume, four are hymns about Krishna, one about Ganesa, two about Kartikeya or Subrahmanya and two relate to the Divine Mother.

राग : भूपाळम् Rāga : Bhoopālam

1. येत्तनै कोडि इन्बं वैत्ताय्-येंगळ्
इऱैवा! इऱैवा! इऱैवा! (ओ-येत्तनै)

चित्तिनै अचित्तुडन् इणैत्ताय्-अंगु
शेरुमैं भूतत्तु वियनुलगमैत्ताय्
अत्तनै उलगमुं वर्णक्कळञ्चिय
मागप्पल पल नल्लऴ् गुशमैत्ताय् (ओ-येत्तनै)

मुक्तियेन्ऱोरु निलैयिनै शमैत्ताय्-अंगु
मुऴु दिनैयुमुणरु मुणर्वमैत्ताय्
भक्तियेन्ऱोरु निलै वगुत्ताय येंगळ्
परमा, परमा, परमा (ओ-येत्तनै)

Ettanai kóḍi inbam vaittai-yéngal
iṛaivā! iṛaivā! iṛaivā! (o-ettanai)

Chittinai achittuḍan iṇaittāi-angu
Śerumaim bhūtattu viyanulagamaittāi
Attanai ulagamum varṇakkalanjīya
Māgap pala pala nallazhagukaḷ śamaittāi (o-ettanai)

Muktiyenṛoru nilaiyinai śamaittai-angu
Muzhudinaiyu muṇarumuṇarvamaittāi
Bhaktiyenṛoru nilai vaguttai yengaḷ
Paramā, paramā, paramā (o-ettanai)

1. Ettanaikodi inbam

How many million sources of joy have you kept for us!

O! God! O! God! Our Lord!

You united the conscious with the unconscious and therein created the world composed of the five elements!

You made the entire world a granary of colour and set up myriad beautiful things!

You created a state called liberation and therein created the consciousness to realise the whole!

You assigned a state named devotion!

O! Supreme Power! O! Supreme Power! Our Supreme Power!

राग : नाट Rāga : Nāṭa

2. कर्पग विनायकक्कडवुळे, पोट्रि!
चिऱ्पर मोनत्तवन् वाऴूग!
वारण मुखत्तान् मलर्त्ताळ् वेल्ग!
आरण मुखत्तान् अरुट्पदं वेल्ग!
पडैप्पुक् किऱैयवन् पण्णवर् नायकन्
इन्दिर गुरुयेनदियत्तोऴिर्वान्
चन्दिर मौलित्तलैवन् मैन्दन्

Kaṛpaga vināyakakkaḍavuḷe poṭṛi!
Chiṛpara monattavan vāzlıga!
Vāraṇa mukhattān malarttaḷ velga!
Āraṇa mukhattān aruṭpadam velga!
Paḍaippukkiṛaiyavan paṇṇavar nāyakan
Indira guru yenadiyattoḷirvān
Chandira moulittalaivan maindan

गणपति ताळै क्करुत्तिडै वैप्पोम्;
गुणमदिर्पलर्वा; कूऱक्केलीर्;
उट्चेवि तिऱक्कुं; अगक्कण् ओळितरुम्;
अग्नि तोन्रुं; आण्मै वलियुरुम्

Gaṇapati tāḷaik karuttiḍai vaippom;
Guṇamadiṛpalavām; kūṛakkeḷīr;
Uṭchevi tiṛakkum; agakkaṇ oḷitarum;
Agni tonṛum; āṇmai valiyuṛum

2. Karpaga Vinayaka

O! Lord Karpaga Vinayaka! Salutations!
O! Lord of great beauty! Hail!
Let the lotus feet of the Elephantfaced One be victorious!
Let the step of the mouthpiece of the Vedas be victorious!
He is the Lord of creation! the Chief of litterateurs!
He is Indra's teacher! who gives radiance to my heart!
He is the son of the crescentcrested Lord!

Let us keep the feet of Ganapati in our thoughts!
There are many benefits in this, please listen!
The inner ears will open, inner eye will give light!
Fire will appear! Manliness will increase!

दिक्केलां वेन्रु जयक्कोडि नाट्टलाम्
कट् चेवि तन्नैक्कैयिले येडुक्कलाम्;
विडत्तैयुं नोवैयुं वेंपकैयदनैयुम्
तुच्चमेन्रेण्णि त्तुयुरिलादिंगु
निच्चलुं वाऌन्दु निलैपेट्रोगलाम्;
अच्चम् तीरुं; अमुदं विळैयुम्;
वित्तै वळरुं; वेव्वि योङ्गुम्;
अमरत्तन्मैयु मेय्दवुम्
इङ्गु नां पेऱलां; इह्दुणर्वीरे

Dikkelām venṛu jayakkoḍi nāṭṭalām
Kaṭchevi tannai kkaiyilé yeḍukkalām;
Viḍattaiyum nóvaiyum vempakaiyadanaiyum
Tuchchamenṛeṇṇit tuyarilādingu
Nichchalum vāzhndu nilaipeṭṛongalām;
Achcham tīrum; amudam vilaiyum;
Vittai vaḷarum; veḷviyongum;
Amarattanmaiyu meidavum
Ingu nām peṛalām; Ihduṇarvīré

We can plant the flag of victory everywhere!

We can safely handle snakes!

Treating poison, disease and enmity as trifles, we can live without sorrow and flourish!

Fear will end, Immortality will prevail! Learning will grow! Penances and sacrifices will flourish!

We can achieve here and now Truth and immortality! Let us realise this!

राग : सिन्धु भैरवी Rāga : Sindhu Bhairavi

3. विल्लिनै योत्त पुरुवं वळैत्तनै,
वेलवा! - अंगोऱ्
वेऱ्पु नोरुंगि प्पोडिप्पोडि
यानतु, वेलवा!
शोल्लिनैत्तेनिऱ् कुऴैत्तुरैप्पाळ् शिऱु
वळ्ळियैक्कण्डु
शोक्कि मरमेन निन्ऱनै तेन्मलै
काट्टिले

Villinai yotta puruvam vaḷaittanai,
Velavā! – angor
Veṛpu norungip poḍippoḍi
Yānatū, velavā!
Śollinait teniṛkkuzhaitturaippāḷ śiṛu
Valliyaikkaṇḍu
Śokki maraména ninṛanai ténmalai
Kāṭṭile

3. Villinaiyotta

O! Lord with the spear! Subrahmanya! You just bent your bowlike brows

And immediately the cause of fear was broken to pieces!

You saw the young girl Valli, who has honeyed speech, in the forests of the southern hills and stood captivated like a tree!

कल्लिनै योत्त वलिय मनङ्कोण्ड
पातकन्-शिंगन्
कण्णिरण्डायिरं काक्कै क्किरैयिट्ट वेलवा!

पल्लिनैक्काट्टि वेण्मुत्तैप्पऴित्तिडुम्
वळ्ळियै-ओरु
पार्प्पनक्कलोलन्तरित्तुक्करन्तोट्ट वेलवा!

Kallinai yotta valiya manankonḍa
Pātakan-śingan
Kaṇṇiraṇḍāyiram kākkaikkiraiyiṭṭa
Velavā

Pallinaikkāṭṭi veṇmuttai ppazhittidum
Vaḷḷiyai-Oru
Pārppana kkólantarittuk karantoṭṭa
Velavā

O! Lord with the spear! You destroyed the two thousand-eyed demon with a heart hard as stone and threw him as food for the crows!

You assumed the form of (an old) brahmin and married Valli whose teeth rival white pearls!

वेळ्ळलैक्कैगळै क्कोट्टि मुलुङ्गुम् कडलिनै-उडल्
वेंबिमरु़गिक्करु़गिप्पुगैय वेरुट्टिनाय्
किळ्ळै मोलि़च्चिरु़वळ्ळियेनुं पेयर् चेल्वत्तै-येन्नुम्
केडट्र् वालि़विनै यिन्ब विळक्कै मरुविनाय्
कोळ्ळै कोण्डे अमरावति वालू़वु कुलैत्तवन्-बानु
कोपन् तलै पत्तुक्कोडि त्तुणुक्कुऱ् कोपित्ताय्
तुळ्ळि क्कुलावित्तिरुयुञ्चिरु़वन् मानैप्पोल्-तिनैत्
तोट्टत्तिलेयोरुपेण्णै मणम् कोण्ड वेलवा!

Veḷḷalaikkaigaḷaik koṭṭi muzhangum kaḍaliani-uḍal
Vembi marugik karugippugaiya veruṭṭināi
Kiḷḷai mozhichchiru vaḷḷiyenum peyar chélavattai-yénṛum
Keḍatra vāzhvinai yinba viḷakkai maruvināi
Koḷḷaikondé amarāvatī vāzhvu kulaittavan-bānu
Gopan talai pattukoḍittuṇukkuṛa kopittāi
Tuḷḷik kulavittiriyunciṛuvan mānaippol-tinait
Tóṭṭattiléyoru peṇṇai maṇam koṇḍa velavā!

You frightened away the ocean with thunderous waves of flooding waters to disappear in smoke getting dry and burnt!

You gave that treasure called Valli, whose speech is sweet as the parrot's, an immortal life and lit up the lamp of bliss.

You scattered in anger into a million smithereens the ten heads of the demon Bhanugopan who plundered and disturbed the life in Amaravati, the capital of Indra.

O! Lord with the spear! You married a girl in the playgardens—a girl who danced and frolicked like a young gazelle.

आऱुशुडर् मुखं कण्डु विऴिक्किन्ब माकुदे; -कैयिल्
अञ्चलेनुं कुऱि कण्डु मगिऴ्चियुण् डाकुदे
नीऱुपडक्कोडुं पावं पिणि पशि यावैयुं-इङ्गु
नीक्कियडियारै नित्तमुं कात्तिडुम् वेलवा!
कूऱु पडप्पल कोडियुणवरिन् कूट्टत्तैक्-कण्डु
कोक्करित्तण्डङ् कुलुङ्ग नकैत्तिडुं शेवलाय्!
माऱुपडप्पल वेऱु वडिवोडु तोन्ऱुवाळ्-येङ्गळ्
वैरवि पेट्ऱ पेरुंगनले वडि वेलवा!

Āṛu śuḍar mukham kaṇḍu vizhikkinba makudé; -kaiyil
Anchalenum kuṛi kaṇḍu magizhchiyuṇ ḍākudé
Nīru paḍakkóḍum pāvam piṇi paśi yāvaiyum-ingu
Nīkkiyaḍaiyārai nittamum kattiḍum velavā!
Kūru paḍappala koḍiyvunavarin kūṭṭattaik-kaṇḍu
Kokkarittanḍan kulunga nagaittiḍum śevalāi!
Māṛu paḍappala veṛu vaḍivoḍu tonṛuvāḷ-yengaḷ
Vairavi peṭra perunganalé vaḍi velavā!

It is blissful to look at your six radiant faces
To see the sign of refuge in your hands gives joy!

O! Lord with the spear! You ever protect us, removing all our sins and diseases and poverty turning them into ashes!

O! Lord with the peacock as your vehicle! You laughed thunderously on seeing the assembled hordes of drummers!

O! Lord with the spear! Subrahmanya! You are the fiery son of our Divine Mother, who has assumed so many diverse forms!

राग : नाट्टकुरिञ्जि Rāga : Nāṭṭakurinji

4. मुरुगा-मुरुगा-मुरुगा
वरुवाय् मयिल्मीदिनिले
वडिवेलुडने वरुवाय्
तरुवाय् नलमुन्तकवुं पुगलुन्
तवमुं तिऱमुं धनमुं गनमुम् (मुरुगा)
अडियार् पलरिङ्गुळरे
अवरै विडुवित्तरुळ्वाय्
मुडिया मऱैयिन् मुडिवे! असुरर्
मुडिवे करुदुं वडिवेलवने! (मुरुगा)
सुरुतिप्पोरुळे, वरुग!
तुणिवे, कनले, वरुग!
करुदिक्करुदिक्कवलैप्पडुवार्
कवलैक्कडलैक्कडियुं वडिवेल् (मुरुगा)

Muruga–Muruga–Muruga
Varuvāi mayilmīdinilé
Vaḍivéludané varuvāi
Taruvāi malamuntagavam pugazhun
Tavamum tiṛamun dhanamum ganamum (Muruga)
Aḍiyār palaringuḷaré
Avarai viḍuvittarulvāi
Muḍiyā maṛain muḍive! asurar
Muḍive karudum vaḍivélavané! (Muruga)
Srutipporulé, varuga!
Tuṇivé, kanalé, varuga!
Karudikarudikavalaippuḍuvār
Kavalaikkaḍalaikkaḍiyum vaḍivel (Muruga)

4. Muruga-Muruga-Muruga

O! Muruga! the Youthful One!

Please come on the peacock

Please come with the spear!

Please give us welfare, goodness, fame, penance, skill and wealth and dignity.

We are many of us here

Please liberate us all!

You are the culmination of the immortal Vedas!

O! Lord with the spear, you always desire the destruction of the demons!

O! Essence of the Vedas! Please come!

O! Embodiment of valour and fiery anger, please come!

O! Lord with the spear! You remove the sea of worries of those who go on worrying!

अमरावतिवाऴ्वुरवे
अरुळ्वाय! शरणं, शरणम्
कुमरा पिणि यावैयुमे शिदऱ्क्
कुमुऱुं शुडर्वेलवने शरणम्

Amarāvati vāzh vuṛavé
Aruḷvāi! śaraṇam, śaraṇam
Kumarā piṇi yāvaiyumé śidaṛak
Kumuṛum śuḍarvélavané śaraṇam

अऱिवागिय कोयिलिले
अरुळागियताय् मडिमेल्
पोऱिवेलुडने वळर्वाय्, अडियार्
पुदु वाऴ्वुरवे पुवि मीदरुळ्वाय्

Aṛivāgiya kóyililé
Aruḷāgiyatāi maḍimél
Poṛivéluḍané vaḷarvāi, aḍiyār
Pudu vāzhvuṛavé puvi mīdaruḷvāi

गुरुवे परमन् मगने,
गुहैयिल् वळरुं कनले,
तरुवाय् तोऴिलुं पयनुं, अमरर्
समराधिपने, शरणं शरणम्

Guruve paraman magané,
Guhaiyil vaḷarum kanalé,
Taruvāi tozhilum payanum amarar
Samarādhipané śaraṇam śaraṇam

Be gracious! O! Lord linked to the capital of Indra, Amaravati! I seek refuge in you, O! Refuge!

O! Kumara! the darling son!

O! Lord with the spear! You scatter away all suffering! I seek refuge in you!

In the temple of knowledge, on the lap of the Mother who is all grace, may you flourish with the sharp spear!

Confer grace on this earth and grant us a new life!

O! Teacher! Son of the Supreme Power!

You, Fire, who grow in the cave!

Give us work and fruit thereof, O! Commander-in-chief of the celestials! I seek refuge in you, O! Refuge!

राग : भीमपलास् Rāga : Bhīmpalās

5. वेळ्ळैत्तामरैप्पूविलिरुप्पाळ्
वीणैशेय्युं ओलियिलिरुप्पाळ्
कोळ्ळै यिन्बं कुलवु कवितै
कूऱु पावलर् उळ्ळत्तिरुप्पाळ्
उळ्ळतां पोरुळ् तेडियुणर्न्दे
ओदुं वेदत्तिनुण्णिन्ऱोळिर्वाळ्
कळ्ळमट्र मुनिवर्कळ् कूऱुम्
करुणै वाचकत्तुट्पोरुळावाळ्।

Veḷḷaittāmaraippūviliruppāḷ
Vīṇai śéyyum oliyiliruppāḷ
Koḷḷaiyinbam kulavu kavitai
Kūṛu pāvalar uḷḷattiruppāḷ
Uḷḷatām póruḷ téḍiyuṇarndé
Ódum vedattinuṇṇinṛoḷirvāḷ
Kaḷḷamaṭra munivargaḷ kūṛum
Karuṇai vāchakattuṭporuḷāvāḷ

5. Vellai Taamarai

She is seated in the lotus flower!
As also in the sound of the lute!

She is seated in the hearts of poets who make blissful poetry!

She shines inside the Vedas which speak of, after enquiry and realisation, the Only Reality, God!

She is the inner meaning of the soothing words of guileless savants.

मातर्तीङ् कुरर्पाट्टिलिरुप्पाळ्
मक्कळ् पेशुं मऴ़लैयिलुळ्ळाळ्
गीतं पाड़ुं कुयिलिन् कुरलै
किळियिनावै यिरुप्पिडङ्कोण्डाळ्
कोद कन्र तोऴ़िलुडैत्तागिक्
कुलवु चित्तिरं गोपुरं कोयिल्
ईदनैत्तिन् येऴ़िलिडैयुट्राळ्
इन्बमे वडिवाकिडप्पेट्राळ्

Mātartīnkurarpāṭṭiliruppāḷ
Makkaḷ péśum mazhalaiyiluḷḷaḷ
Gītam pāḍum kuyilin kuralai
Kiḷiyināvai yiruppiḍankoṇḍāḷ
Koda kanṛa tozhiluḍaittagik
Kulavu chittiram gópuram kóyil
Īdanaittin yezhiliḍaiyuṭṛaḷ
Inbamé vaḍivākiḍappetṛaḷ

She is in the sweet voices of women

as also in the lispings of children!

She takes her seat on the tongues of koels which sing sweet songs!

She is the basis of beauty in fruitful work, shining pictures and temple towers!

She is the embodiment of bliss!

राग : पूर्ण चन्द्रिका Rāga : Poorna Chandrikā

6. वरुवाय्, वरुवाय्, वरुवाय् - कण्णा
वरुवाय्, वरुवाय्, वरुवाय्

Varuvāi, varuvāi, varuvāi - Kaṇṇā
Varuvāi, varuvāi, varuvāi

वरुवाय् अऱिविल् ओळिर्वाय् - कण्णा
उयिरिन्नमुदाय् पोऴिवाय् - कण्णा
वरुवाय् येन्नुळ् वळर्वाय् - कण्णा
कमलत्तिरुवोडिणैवाय् - कण्णा (वरुवाय्)

Varuvāi aṛivil oḷirvāi - Kaṇṇā
Uyirinnamudāi pozhivāi - Kaṇṇā
Varuvāi yennuḷ vaḷarvāi - Kaṇṇā
Kamalattiruvoḍiṇaivāi - Kaṇṇā (Varuvāi)

इणैवाय् येनदावियिले - कण्णा
इदयत्तिनिले यमर्वाय् - कण्णा
कणैवायशुरर् तलैकळ् - शिदऱ्
कडैयूऴियिले पडैयोडेऴुवाय्! (वरुवाय्)

Iṇaivāi yenadāviyilé - Kaṇṇā
Idayattinilé yamarvāi - Kaṇṇā
Kaṇaivāyaśurar talaikaḷ - Śidaṛ
Kaḍaiyūzhiyilé paḍaiyoḍezhuvāi! (Varuvāi)

6. Varuvai Varuvai

Come, come, come, O! Krishna
Come, come, come!
Come embodied, as the light in knowledge, Krishna!
As the shower of immortality to life! O! Krishna!
Grow in me as the building block, O! Krishna!
Ever united with Lakshmi, the Lotus Mother! O! Krishna!

Get merged with my lifebreath, O! Krishna!
Be seated in my heart, O! Krishna!
Be the arrow to kill and scatter the hordes of demons!
Come with the hordes of your troops at the time of deluge!

येलुवाय् कडल् मीदिनिले - येलुमोर्
इरविक्किणैया उळमीदिनिले
तोलुवेन् शिवनां निनैये - कण्णा,
तुणैये, अमरर् तोलुं वानवने! (वरुवाय्)

Yezhuvāi kaḍal mīdinile - yezhumór
Iravikkiṇaiya uḷamīdinilé
Tozhuvén śivanām ninaiye - Kaṇṇā
Tuṇaiye, amarar tozhum vānavané! (Varuvāi)

Rise, like the sun which rises over the ocean, in my mind!

O! Krishna! I worship you, who are also Siva!

You are my refuge, O! Heavenly Being venerated by the angels!

राग : कल्याण वसन्तम् Rāga : Kalyāna Vasantam

7. काक्कैचि्चऱ्गिनिले नन्दलाला – निन्ऱन्
करियनिऱन्तोन्ऱुदैये नन्दलाला;

पाक्कुं मरंगळेल्लां नन्दलाला – निन्ऱन्
पच्चै निऱन्तोन्ऱुदैये नन्दलाला;

केट्कुमोलियिलेल्लां नन्दलाला – निन्ऱन्
गीतमिशैक्कुतडा नन्दलाला;

तीक्कुळ् विरलैवैत्ताल् नन्दलाला – निन्नैत्
तीण्डुंमिन्बन्तोन्ऱुतडा नन्दलाला॥

Kākkaichchiṛaginilé nandalālā - ninṛan
Kariya niṛantónṛudaiyé nandalālā;

Parkkum marangaḷéllām nandalālā - ninṛan
Pachchai nirantonṛudaiyé nandalālā;

Keṭkumoliyiléllām nandalālā - ninṛan
Gītamiśaikkutaḍā nandalālā;

Tīkkuḷ viralai vaittāl nandalālā - ninnait
Tīṇḍuminbantonrutaḍā nandalālā//

7. Kakkai Siraginile

O! Son of Nanda! I see your dark colour in the wings of the dark crow!

I see your green colour in all the trees that I see!

Your songs resonate in all the sounds that I hear!
O! Son of Nanda, Sri Krishna!

When I put my finger in the fire, I feel the bliss of touching you!
O! Son of Nanda!

राग : माण्ड् बहार् Rāga : Mānḍ Bahār

8. कायिले पुळिप्पदेन्ने ? कण्ण पेरुमाने ! - नी
कनियिले इनिप्पदेन्ने ? कण्ण पेरुमाने !
नोयिले पडुप्पदेन्ने ? कण्ण पेरुमाने ! - नी
नोन्बिले उयिर्प्पदेन्ने ? कण्ण पेरुमाने !
काट्रिले कुळिर्न्ददेन्ने ? कण्ण पेरुमाने ! - नी
कनलिले शुडुवदेन्ने ? कण्ण पेरुमाने !
शेट्रिले कुऴंबलेन्ने ? कण्ण पेरुमाने ! - नी
दिक्किले तेळिन्ददेन्ने ? कण्ण पेरुमाने !
येट्रि निन्नैत्तोऴुवदेन्ने ? कण्ण पेरुमाने ! - नी
येळियर्तंमैक्काप्पदेन्ने ? कण्ण पेरुमाने !
पोट्रिनोरै क्काप्पदेन्ने ? कण्ण पेरुमाने ! - नी
पोय्यर्तंमै माय्प्पदेन्ने ? कण्ण पेरुमाने !
पोट्रि ! पोट्रि ! पोट्रि ! पोट्रि ! कण्ण पेरुमाने ! - निन्
पोन्नडिकळ् पोट्रि निन्रेन्, कण्ण पेरुमाने !

Kāyilé puḷippadenné? Kaṇṇa perumāné! - nī
Kaniyilé inippadenné? Kaṇṇa perumāné!
Noyilé paḍuppadenné? Kaṇṇa perumāné! - nī
Nonbilé uyirppadenné? Kaṇṇa perumāné!
Kāṭṛilé kuḷirndadenné? Kaṇṇa perumāné! - nī
Kanalilé śuḍuvadenné? Kaṇṇa perumāné!
Śeṭṛilé kuzhambalenné? Kaṇṇa perumāné! - nī
Dikkilé teḷindadenné? Kaṇṇa perumāné!
Yeṭṛi ninnai tozhuvadenné? Kaṇṇa perumāné! - nī
Yeḷiyartammaikkāppadenné? Kaṇṇa perumāné!
Poṭṛinoraikkāppadenné? Kaṇṇa perumāné! - nī
Poyyartammai māippadenné? Kaṇṇa perumāné!
Poṭṛi, poṭṛi, poṭṛi, poṭṛi! Kaṇṇa perumāné! - nin
Ponnaḍikaḷ poṭṛi ninṛen, Kaṇṇa perumāné!

8. Kaayile pulippadenne

O! Lord Krishna! Why do you taste sour in the unripe fruit?

Why do you taste sweet in the ripe fruit? O! Lord Krishna!

Why do you lie down when you are sick? O! Lord Krishna!

Why do you come alive in religious rituals? O! Lord Krishna!

Why are you cool in the wind? O! Lord Krishna!

Why are you hot in fire? O! Lord Krishna!

Why are you messy in dirt? O! Lord Krishna!

Why are you clear on the horizon? O! Lord Krishna!

Why do we raise you on a pedestal and bow to you? O! Lord Krishna!

Why do you protect the lowly and downcast? O! Lord Krishna!

Why do you protect those who worship you? O! Lord Krishna!

Why do you destroy the untruthful? O! Lord Krishna!

Salutations to you again and again! O! Lord Krishna!

I worship your golden feet, O! Lord Krishna!

रागमालिका Rāgamālikā

सिन्धु भैरवी Sindhu Bhairavi

9. तीराद विळैयाट्टुप्पिळ्ळै – कण्णन्
तेरुविले पेण्कळुक्कोयात तोल्लै (तीराद)

तिन्नप्पऌं कोण्डुतरुवान्; – पादि
तिन्किन्र पोदिले तट्टिप्परिप्पान्;
येन्नप्पन् येन्नैयन् येन्राल् – अदनै
येच्चिऱ्पडुत्तिक्कडित्तुक्कोडुप्पान् (तीराद)

बिलहरि Bilahari

तेनोत्त पण्डंकळ् कोण्डु – येन्न
शेय्दालुं येट्टाद उयरत्तिल् वैप्पान्
मानोत्त पेण्णडि येन्बान् – शट्रु
मन मगिलुनेरत्तिले किळ्ळिविडुवान् (तीराद)

Tīrāda viḷaiyāṭṭuppiḷḷai - kaṇṇan
Téruvilé peṇkaḷukkóyāta tollai (Tīrāda)

Tinnappazham koṇḍu taruvān; - pādi
Tinkinra podilé taṭṭippaṛippān;
Ennappan, ennaiyan, yenṛāl - adanai
Echiṛ paḍuttikkaḍittuk koḍuppān (Tīrāda)

Ténotta paṇḍankaḷ koṇḍu - yenna
Śeidalum yeṭṭāda uyarattil vaippān
Mānotta peṇṇaḍi yenbān - śatṛu
Mana magizhu nérattilé kiḷḷiviḍuvān (Tīrāda)

9. Teeraatavilayaattupillai

An endlessly playful child is He-Krishna!

He is a source of endless trouble for the girls in the street!

He will bring fruits to eat, but snatch them away when they are eating halfway!

If they cry "O! Lord! O! dear!", He will bite it and give it.

He will bring eatables sweet as honey, but keep them at an inaccessible height!

"You are like a gazelle" he will say and when she sits happy will pinch her!

षण्मुखप्रिया Shanmukhapriyā

अऴगुळ्ळ मलर्कोण्डु वन्दे - येन्नै
अऴ अऴच्चेय्दु पिन् "कण्णै मूडिक्कोळ्;
कुऴलिले शूट्टुवेन्" येन्बान् - येन्नै
कुरुडाक्कि मलरिनै त्तोऴिक्कु वैप्पान् (तीराद)

Azhagulla malarkondu vande - yennai
Azha-azha cheidu pin "kannai mūdikkol;
Kuzhalilé śūṭṭuvén" yenbān - yennai
Kuruḍākki malarinai tozhikku vaippān (Tīrāda)

माण्ड् Mānḍ

पिन्नलैप्पिन्निन्ऱिऴुप्पान; - तलै
पिन्ने तिरुंबु मुन्ने शेन्ऱु मऱैवान्;
वन्नप्पुदुच्चेलै तनिले - पुऴुदि
वारिच्चोरिन्दे वरुत्तिक्कुऴैप्पान् (तीराद)

Pinnalaippinninṛizhuppān; - talai
Pinné tirumbu munné śenṛu maṛaivān;
Vannappuduchchélai tanile - puzhudi
Vārichchorindé varuttikkuzhaippān (Tīrāda)

He will bring beautiful flowers and after making me cry, he'll say: "Close your eyes! I will set them on your hair." After making me blind, he will put the flowers on my companion's hair!

An endlessly playful child is He-Krishna!

He will pull my pigtail from behind

and hide himself before I turn my head!

On my colourful new dress, he will throw dust and make a mess!

हिन्दोळम् Hindoḷam

पुल्लाङ्कुऴल् कोण्डु वरुवान; - अमुदु
पोङ्गि तदुंबु नऱ्गीतं पडिप्पान्;
कळ्ळाल् मयङ्गुवतुपोले - अदै
कण्मूडि वाय् तिऱन्दे केट्टिरुप्पोम् (तीराद)

देश Desh

अङ्गान्तिरुक्कुं वाय् तनिले - कण्णन्
आरेऴुकट्टेरुं बैप्पोट्टुविडुवान्;
येङ्गागिलुं पार्त्ततुण्डो? - कण्णन्
येङ्गळै च्चेय्किन्र वेडिक्कैयन्रो? (तीराद)

Pullānkuzhal koṇḍu varuvān; - amudu
Pongi tadumbu naṛgītam paḍippān;
Kaḷḷāl mayanguvadu pole - adai
Kaṇmūḍi vāi tiṛandé keṭṭiruppóm (Tīrāda)

Angāntirukkum vāi tanilé - kaṇṇan
Ārézhu kaṭṭeṛumbaippoṭṭuviḍuvān;
Yengāgilum pārttatuṇḍo? - kaṇṇan
Yengaḷai ccheiginṛa veḍikkaiyanṛó? (Tīrāda)

He will bring the flute and play ambrosial music!

And as if drunk with wine, we will listen, our eyes closed and mouths open!

And here and there he will put live ants into the open mouths!
Has anyone seen pranks like the ones Krishna plays on us?

तोडि Toḍi

विळैयाड वावेन्रलैप्पन्; वीट्टिल्
वेलैयेन्रालदैक्केळादिलुप्पान्;
इळैयारोडाडिक्कुदिप्पान्; येम्मै
इडैयिर्पिरिन्दु पोय् वीट्टिले शोल्वान् (तीराद)

काफी Kāfi

अंमैक्कु नल्लवन् , कण्डीर! मूळि
अत्तैक्कु नल्लवन् , तन्दैक्कु मह्दे,
येंमैत्तुयर् शेय्युं पेरियोर् - वीट्टिल्
यावर्क्कु नल्लवन् पोले नडप्पान् (तीराद)

मध्यमावती Madhyamāvati

कोळुक्कु मिगवुञ्चमर्त्तन्; पोय्मै
कुत्तिरं पलिशोलक्कूशा च्चलक्कन्;
आळुक्किशैन्दपडि पेशि - तेरुविल्
अत्तनै पेण्कळैयु माका तडिप्पान् (तीराद)

Viḷaiyāḍa vāvenṛazhaippān; vīṭṭil
Velaiyenṛāladai kkeḷadizhuppān;
Iḷaiyāroḍāḍikkudippān; yemmai
Iḍaiyiṛ pirindupoi vīṭṭile śolvān (Tīrāda)

Ammaikku nallavan, kaṇḍīr! mūḷi
Attaikku nallavan, tandaikku mahdé,
Yemmaittuyar śeyyum periyór - vīṭṭil
Yavarkku nallavan polé naḍappān (Tīrāda)

Koḷukku migavunchamarttan; poimai
Kuttiram pazhiśolakkūśāchchazhakkan;
Āḷukkiśaindapaḍi péśi - teruvil
Attanai peṇkaḷaiyumākā taḍippān (Tīrāda)

He will invite us to play with him

and drag us from household work

He will merrily play with the youngsters

and go home leaving us in the lurch!

He will act as a good boy to his mother!

to his aunt and to his father

He will act as a good boy before all the elders in the house

He is very clever in backbiting

He is shamelessly wicked in speaking lies, deceit and carrying tales

He will speak to each according to her taste and trouble all the girls in the street!

An endlessly playful child is He-Krishna!

राग : पुन्नागवराळी Rāga : Punnāgavarāḷī

10. निन्नैच्चरणडैन्देन् – कण्णंमा!
निन्नैच्चरणडैन्देन्!

पोन्नै उयर्वैप्पुगऴै विरुंबिडुम्
येन्नैक्कवलैकळ् तिन्नत्तगातेन्रु (निन्नै)

मिडिमैयुमच्चमु मेवियेन्नेञ्चिर्
कुडिमै पुगुन्तन, कोन्रवै पोक्केन्रु (निन्नै)

तन् शेयलेण्णि त्तविप्पतु तीन्दिंगु
निन् शेयल् शेय्तु निऱैवु पेरुंवणम् (निन्नै)

Ninnaichcharaṇaḍaindén - kaṇṇammā!
Ninnaichcharaṇaḍaindén!

Ponnai uyarvaippugazhai virumbiḍum
Yennaikkavalaikaḷ tinnattagādenṛu (Ninnai)

Miḍimaiyumachchamu meviyennenchir
Kuḍimai puguntana, konṛavaipókkenru (Ninnai)

Tan śeyaleṇṇittavippatu tīrndingu
Nin śeyal śeitu niṛaivu peṛum vaṇam (Ninnai)

10. Ninnai saranadainthen

I have sought refuge in you, O! Kannamma! My family Deity!

I have sought refuge in you so that worries should not eat me up in the pursuit of gold, position and fame!

Poverty and fear have encroached and entered my mind. To kill them and send them away, I have sought refuge in you, O! Kannamma! My family Deity!

I want to end this suffering caused by my actions, instead, I want to do your bidding and be happy. Hence I have sought refuge in you!

तुन्बमिनियिल्लै, शोर्विल्लै, तोर्पिल्लै,
अन्बु नेरियिल् अरङ्गळ् वळर्त्तिड (निन्नै)

नल्लतु तीयतु नामरियोमन्नै!
नल्लतु नाट्टुक! तीमैयै योट्टुक! (निन्नै)

Tunbaminiyillai, śórvillai, tóṛpillai,
Anbu neṛiyil aṛangaḷ vaḷarttiḍa (Ninnai)

Nallatu tīyatu nāmaṛiyómannai!
Nallatu nāṭṭuka! tīmaiyai yoṭṭuka! (Ninnai)

No more suffering! No more tiredness! No more defeat!

In the path of love, let virtuous deeds grow. Hence it is that I have sought refuge in you!

O! Mother! we do not know what is good and what is evil!

You establish the righteous and banish evil!

I have sought refuge in you, O! Mother Kannamma!

SONGS OF PAPANASAM SIVAN

(19th-20th Century A.D.)

	Song	*Rāga*
1.	Moolaadhaaramoorti	Hamsadhwani
2.	Kaana kan kodivendum	Kamboji
3.	Enna tavam seidanai	Kafi
4.	Kapali	Mohanam
5.	Mahalakshmi	Sankarabharanam
6.	Nee irangaayenil	Athana
7.	Paratpara	Vachaspati
8.	Ka va va	Varali
9.	Nambi kettavar	Hindolam
10.	Karpagame	Madhyamavati

PAPANASAM SIVAN

PAPANASAM SIVAN (26 September 1890-
1 October 1973 A.D.)

Papanasam Sivan, the Tamil music composer, has been termed "Tamil Tyagaraja".

His musical compositions, mainly in Tamil and numbering over 2000, are surcharged with devotion to God in His various manifestations.

He was born in Polagam village in Thanjavur district.

His original name was Ramaiah, and in many of his songs, he has inserted his pen-name as "Ramadasa". But because he lived for some time in Papanasam and was attired like a Saivite devotee, wearing *rudraksha* and holy ashes, he came to be known as "Papanasam Sivan".

Sivan was fond of conducting Bhajans and visited the various temples of Tamil Nadu, singing soul-stirring songs.

From 1930, he started living in Mylapore Madras. He was specially attached to the Lord in the Kapali temple and many of his most heartrending devotional songs centre around the Deities in this temple: *Lord Kapali* and *Mother Karpagam.*

Sivan lived upto the age of 83 years and kept himself busy composing and singing the glories of his beloved Deities. He freely mixed Sanskrit with Tamil in his songs, which are a perfect combination of *Bhakti, Rāga, Sangeeta* and *Sāhitya.*

राग : हंसध्वनि Rāga : Hamsadhwani

1. मूलाधार मूर्त्ति ग़जमुखने शरणं उनदु उभय शरणम् (मूला)

वेलायुध गुहन् तनक्कु मुन् तोन्रिय
विमला उमैयाळ् तरुमगने
अमला येमैयाळ् मुनिवर् तोलुम् (मूला)

अन्बुडन् तुम्बै यरुगं पुल्लै येडुत्
तरुच्चनै चेय्दालुं पोदुम् - अन्बर्
तुन्बं तुडैत्तुप्पेरिन्बम् तरुं वरदा
तुणै पुरि प्रणवाकार गणपतिये (मूला)

Mūlādhāra mūrti gajamukhané śaraṇam
unadu ubhaya śaraṇam (Mūlā)

Velāyudha guhan tanakku mun tónriya
Vimalā umaiyāḷ taru magané
Amalā emaiyāḷ munivar tozhum (Mūlā)

Anbuḍan tumbai yarugam pullai yéḍut
Taruchchanai cheydālum podum - anbar
Tunbam tuḍaittuppérinbam tarum varadā
Tuṇai puri praṇavākāra gaṇapatiyé (Mūlā)

1. Moolaadhaara Murti

O! Elephantfaced One! embodied in Mooladhara!

I seek refuge in your two feet.

Born before Guha, the holder of the spear,

You are the Holy son of Uma, the stainless One!

The pure minded sages bow to you!

Even if worshipped with *tumbai* and *arugam grass** but with love

You remove sorrow and bestow bliss! O! Granter of boons!

Help me O! Ganapati! who is in the form of Pranava (Aum).

O! Elephantfaced One! embodied in Mooladhara! I seek refuge in your two feet.

*Easily available weeds.

राग : कांबोजि Rāga : Kāmboji

2. काणक्कण् कोडि वेण्डुं - कापालियिन् भवनि
काणक्कण् कोटि वेण्डुम्

माणिक्कं वैरं मुतल् नवरत्नाभरणमुम्
मणमार् पऱ्पल मलर् मालैकळुं मुखमुम्
मतियोटु तारागणं निऱैयुं अन्ति
वानमो कमलवनमो येन मनम्
मयङ्ग अकळङ्क अङ्कं यावुं-इ-
लङ्क अपाङ्ग अरुण्मऴै पोऴि भवनि (काणक्)

Kāṇakkaṇkoḍi veṇḍum - kāpāliyin bhavani
Kāṇakkaṇkoṭi veṇḍum

Māṇikkam vairam mutal navaratnābharaṇamum
Maṇamār paṛpala malar mālaikaḷum mukhamum
Matiyoṭu tārāgaṇam niṛaiyum anti
Vānamo kamalavanamo yena manam
Mayanga akaḷanka ankam yāvum-i-
Lanka apānga aruṇmazhai pózhi bhavani (Kāṇak)

2. Kaanakankodi vendum

I need a million eyes to see the splendorous procession of Lord Kapali!

He wears the nine gems like ruby, diamond etc

Many garlands of fragrant flowers

His face resembles the night sky lit by the moon and the stars

Or the cluster of lotuses

So thinks my magnetised mind!

He is the One with faultless limbs

Showering the rain of grace!

One needs a million eyes to see the resplendent procession of Lord Kapali!

मालोडयन् पणियुं मण्णुं विण्णुं परवुम्
मऱ़ै यागमन्तुतिक्कुं इऱ़ैवन् अरुळ् पेऱ़वे
कालञ्चेल्लुमुन् कनधनमुन्तन्तार्क्कु नन्ऱ़ि-
करुतिक्कण्णारक् कण्डुळ् ळुरुकिप्पणियप्पलर्
काण अरुमुखनुं गणपतियु ञ्चण्-
डेश्वरनुं शिवगणमुन्तोडरक्कलै-
वाणि तिरुवुं पणि कऱ़्पक नायकि-
वामन् अधिकारनन्दि सेवैतनैक् (काणक्)

Mālóḍayan paṇiyum maṇṇum viṇṇum paravum
Maraiyāgamantutikkum iṛaivan aruḷ peṛavé
Kālanchellumun kanadhanamuntantārkku nanṛi-
Karutikkaṇṇārak kaṇḍuḷ ḷurukippaṇiyappalar
Kāṇa arumukhanum gaṇapatiyunchaṇ-
Ḍeśwaranum śivagaṇamuntoḍarkkaḷai-
Vāṇi tiruvum paṇi kaṛpaka nāyaki-
Vāman adhikāranandi śevaitanaik (Kāṇak)

Vishnu and Brahma bow to Him, Vedas which pervade the heaven and earth, praise Him.

To obtain His grace,

Before the time is over, to express gratitude to the Lord who grants boundless wealth.

Many see Him eyeful and bow with melting hearts.

Accompanied by Subrahmanya, Ganesa, Chanteeswara and the Ganas and Mother Karpaga, to whom Saraswati and Rama bow, and served by the powerful bull, Nandi,

He comes.

One needs a million eyes to see the splendorous procession of Lord Kapali!

राग : काफी | Rāga : Kāfī

3. येन्न तवं शेय्दनै यशोदा
येङ्गुं निऱै पर ब्रह्मं अंमा येन्ऱलैक्क (येन्न)

ईरेलु भुवनङ्कळ् पटैत्तवनैक् कैयिलेन्ति
शीराट्टि पालूट्टि तालट्टिट (येन्न)

ब्रह्मनुं इन्दिरनुं मनतिल् पोऱामै कोळ्ळ
उरलिल् कट्टि वाय् पोत्तिक् केञ्च वैत्ताय् ताये (येन्न)

सनकातियर् तव योगं शेय्तु साधित्ततै
पुनितमाते येळितिल् पेऱ् (येन्न)

Enna tavam śeidanai yaśodā
Engum niṛai para brahmam ammā enṛazhaikka (enna)

Īrezhu bhuvanankaḷ paṭaittavanaik kaiyilénti
Śīrāṭṭi pālūṭṭi tālaṭṭiṭa (enna)

Brahmanum indiranum manatil poṛāmai koḷḷa
Uralil kaṭṭi vāi pottik kencha vaittāi tāyé (enna)

Sanakātiyar tava yogam śeitu sādhittatai
Punitamāté eḷitil pera (enna)

3. Enna tavam seidanai

O! Mother Yasoda! What penance did you do?

So that the all-pervading Supreme Power could call you "Mother"!

Him, who created the fourteen worlds, you took in your hand, caressed, fed with milk and sang lullabies to!

What penance did you do, Yasoda?

Inciting the jealousy of Brahma and Indra,

You tied Him to a pestle and made Him beg you with mouth shut,

What penance did you do, Yasoda!

What Sages like Sanaka could achieve with hard spiritual practices

O! Holy Mother! you could achieve so easily!

What penance did you do, Yasoda?

राग : मोहनम् Rāga : Mohanam

4. कपालि, करुणैनिलवुपोऴि वदन मदियनोरु (कपालि)

आबाल गोपालम् आऴिशूऴ् तलत्तवरुम्
भूपालरुं अष्टदिक्पालरुं पोट्रुं अद्भुत (कपालि)

मति पुनल् अरवुकोन्रै तुम्बै अरुकुन्
मत्तै पुनै माशडैयान्
विदितलैमालै मार्बन् उरित्तकरियिन्
वेम्बुलियिन् तोलुडैयान्
अदिर मुऴङ्गुम् उडुक्कैयुं तिरिशूलमुम्
अङ्गियुं कुरङ्गमुं इलङ्गिडु कैयान्
द्युतिमिगु तिरुमेनि मुऴुदुं शांबल्
तुलङ्ग येदिर्मङ्गैयर् मनंकवर् जगन्मोहन (कपालि)

Kapāli, karuṇai nilavu pozhi vadana madiyanoru (Kapāli)

Ābāla Gopālam āzhiśoozh talattavarum
Bhūpālarum aṣṭadikpālarum póṭrum adbhuta (Kapāli)

Mati punal aravukonṛai tumbai aṛukun
Mattai punai māśaḍaiyān
Viditalaimālai mārban urittakariyin
Vémbuliyin tóluḍaiyān
Adira muzhangum uḍukkaiyum tiriśūlamum
Angiyum kurangamum ilangiḍu kaiyān
Dyutimigu tiruméni muzhudum śāmbal
Tulanga yedirmangaiyar manam kavar Jaganmohana (Kapāli)

4. Kapali

O! Kapali! Your face is like the moon. Please shed the moonlight of mercy.

You, wondrous One, are praised by all: from children to rulers and sages, those who protect the earth and those who guard the quarters.

You wear the crescent moon, Ganga, snakes and flowers like *kondrai, tumbai* and *umattai* and *arugam grass* on your matted hair.

You wear as garland Brahma's head!

You wear the skin of the elephant and the tiger!

You hold the trident and the resounding drum!

Your hands shine with fire and the deer.

Your entire lustrous body is smeared with ashes.

You win the hearts of all women, O! Enticer of the universe!

O! Kapali whose face is like the moon! Please shed the moonlight of mercy!

राग : शंकराभरणम् Rāga : Śankarābharaṇam

5. महा लक्ष्मि जगन्माता
मनमिरङ्गि वरमरुळ् (महा)

महा विष्णुविन् मार्बेनुं
मणि पीठमदनिल् अमर्न्दरुळ्
मन्मथनै ईन्ररुळुं ताये
दया निधिये महा माये (महा)

पार्कडल् तरुं कृपा करि
परिन्दु वन्देमै आदरि
पंकज मलर् वळर् अन्नैये - कडैक्कण्
पार् रामदासन् पणियुं (महा)

Mahā lakṣmi jaganmātā
Manamirangi varamaruḷ (Mahā)

Mahāviṣṇuvin mārbenum
Maṇi pīṭhamadanil amarndaruḷ
Manmathanai īnraruḷum tāyé
Dayānidhiyé mahā māyé (Mahā)

Pāṛ kaḍal tarum krupā kari
Parindu vandemai ādari
Pankaja malar vaḷar annaiyé - kaḍaikkaṇ
Pāṛ Rāma dāsan paṇiyum (Mahā)

5. Mahalakshmi

O! Mahalakshmi! O! Mother of the universe!

Melt your mind and grant me grace!

You sit on the bejewelled throne, which is the Great Vishnu's chest!

O! Mother! who bless Cupid, the god of love!

O! Treasurehouse of mercy! Great Mother!

O! Mahalakshmi! O! Mother of the universe!

O! Creatrix of kindness, bequeathed by the Milky Ocean!

Be indulgent to us and bless us!

O! Mother seated on the lotus flower! Cast your glance on us! Ramadasan bows to you.

O! Mahalakshmi! Mother of the universe!

Melt your mind and grant us grace!

राग : अठाणा Rāga : Aṭhāṇā

6. नी इऱ्ङ्गायेनिल् पुगलेदु अम्ब
निखिल जगन्नाथन् मार्बिल् उऱै तिरु (नी)

Nī irangāyenil pugalédu amba
Nikhila jagannāthan mārbil uṛai tiru (Nī)

तायिरङ्गाविडिल् शेयुयिर् वालुमो
सकल उलगिऱ्कुं नी तायल्लवो – अंब (नी)

Tāyirangāviḍil śeyuyir vāzhumó
Sakala ulagiṛkum nī tāyallavó - amba (Nī)

पाऱ्कडलिल् उदित्त तिरुमणिये – सौ
भाग्य लक्ष्मि यैन्नै क्कडैक्कणिये
नाऱ्कवियुं पोऴियुं पुलवोर्क्कुं –मेय्
ज्ञानियर्क्कुं उयर् वानवर्क्कुं अम्ब (नी)

Pāṛ kaḍalil uditta tirumaṇiyé - sow
Bhāgya lakṣmi yennaik kaḍaikkaṇiyé
Nāṛkaviyum pozhiyum pulavórkkum - mei
Gnāniyarkkum uyar vānavarkkum amba (Nī)

6. Nee Irangayenil

If you do not show mercy to me, where is my refuge, O! Mother!
Who ever stays on the chest of the Lord of the whole universe.
If the mother does not show mercy, how can the child survive?
Aren't you the mother for all the worlds?
O! Holy gem who arose out of the milky ocean!
O! Auspicious Lakshmi! glance at me!
You are the mother of the sages who recite the four Vedas!
as also of the realised souls and the high celestials of heaven.
If you do not show mercy to me, where is my refuge, Mother?

राग : वाचस्पति

Rāga : Vāchaspati

7. परात्परा परमेश्वरा पार्वतीपते हर पशुपते (परात्)

Parātparā paraméśwarā pārvatīpaté
Hara paśupaté (Parāt)

सुरा सुरर् तोलुं पावन सुन्दर चरणारविन्द आनन्द (परात्)

Surāsurar tozhum pāvana sundara
charaṇāravinda ānanda (Parāt)

अरिययनुं काणवरिय जोति
आदियन्तमिल्ला प्पलुमनादिप्
पुरमेरित्त मुक्कट्करुम्बे येन्तन्
पुण्यमूर्त्ति सुब्रह्मण्यन् तन्दैये (परात्)

Ariyayanum kāṇavariya jóti
Ādiyantamillāp pazhamanādip
Purameritta mukkaṭkarumbé yéntan
Puṇyamūrtti subrahmaṇyan tandaiyé (Parāt)

7. Paratpara

O! Supreme among the gods! O! Supreme Lord! O! Lord of Parvati! O! Lord of all creatures!

O! Handsome, blissful One with lotus feet, who is worshipped by both angels and demons!

O! Radiance, which could not be seen even by Hari and Brahma! O! Primordial One without beginning or end!

O! Destroyer of Tripura! from whom the Trinity have sprouted!

My auspicious Deity! Father of Subrahmanya!

राग : वराळी Rāga : Varāḷī

8. का वा वा कन्दा वा वा येनैक्का वा वेला वा
पऴ्नि मलै युऱैयु मुरुगा (का)

Kā vā vā kandā vā vā yenaikkā vā velā vā
Pazhani malai yuṛaiyu muruga (Kā)

देवादि देवन् मगने वा-परदेवि मडियिलमरुं गुहने वा वळ्ळि-
देय्वयानै मणवाळा वा-शरवण भव परम दयाळा षण्मु (का)

Dévādi dévan magané vā-paradévi
madiyilamarum guhané vā vaḷḷi-
Deivayānai maṇavāḷā vā śaravaṇa bhava
parama dayāḷā shaṇmu (Kā)

आबत्तिरुळर् अरुळोळि तरुं अप्पने अण्णले ऐय्या वा
पापत्तिरळ् तरुंतापं अगल वरुंपऴ्निवळर् करुणै मऴैये वा
तापत्रय वेयिलर् निऴल् तरुंवान् तरुवे येन् कुल गुरुवे वा
श्रीपद्मनाभन् मरुगा रामदासन् वणङ्गुं मुत्तय्या विरैवोडु (का)

Ābattiruḷaṛa aruḷoḷi tarum appané aṇṇalé aiyā vā
Pāpattiraḷ tarum tāpam agala varum pazhani
valar karuṇai mazhaiyé vā
Tāpatraya veyilaṛa nizhal tarum vān taruvé en kula
guruvé vā
Śrī padmanābhan marugā rāmadāsan vaṇangum
muttaiya viraivoḍu
(Kā)

8. Ka va va

Come to protect me O! Skanda! Holder of the spear! Come, come to protect me!

O! youthful Lord, who resides in the Palani hill!

Come, O! Son of the Lord of gods!

Come, O! Guha, who sits on the lap of the Supreme Goddess!

Come, Husband of Valli and Devayani!

O! Six-faced One! born of the Saravana pond! O! Supremely Compassionate One!

Come, come to protect me!

Come! O! Lord! O! God! O! Father! Who gives the light of grace in the darkness of difficulties!

Come! O! Resident of Palani hill! Who showers the rain of mercy to remove the drought of the burden of sins!

Come! O! My family Deity! The heavenly tree who gives the cool shade to save from the sunlight of the three tortures!

Come fast! O! My jewel of a Lord! Nephew of Sri Padmanabha, to whom Ramadasa bows.

राग : हिन्दोळम् Rāga : Hindoḷam

9. नंबिक्केट्टवर् येवर् ऐय्या - उमै
नायकनैत् तिरुमयिलैयिन् इऱैवनै (नंबिक्)

Nambikkeṭṭavar evaraiyā - umai
Nāyakanait tirumayilaiyin iṛaivanai (Nambik)

अंबुलि गङ्गै अणिन्द जटाधरन्
अन्बर् मनं वळर् शंभु कपालियै (नंबिक्)

Ambuli gangai aṇinda jaṭādharan
Anbar manam vaḷar śambhu kapāliyai (Nambik)

ओन्रुमे पयन् इल्लैयेन्रु उणर्न्दपिन्बवर् उण्डेन्बार्
ओव्वोरुमनिदनुं ओरुनाळ् इन्निलै येय्दुरुदि इदै मऱन्दार्
अन्रु शेयलिलुन्दल मरुपोलुदु शिवन् पेयर् नाविल् वरादे
आदलिनाल् मनमे इन्रे शिल नामं शोल्लिप्पलगु अन्बुडन् (नंबिक्)

Onṛumé payan illaiyenṛu uṇarnda pinbavar uṇḍenbār
Ovvoru manidanum orunāḷ innilai yeyduṛudi idai maṛandār
Anṛu śéyalizhandala maṛu pozhudu śivan péyar nāvil varādé
Ādalināl manamé inṛé śila nāmam śollippazhagu anbuḍan
(Nambik)

9. Nambi kettavar

O! Lord! Who has trusted in you and gone astray?

O! Lord of Uma! O! God who resides in holy Mylai!

Who has trusted in you and gone astray?

O! Lord who wears the moon and the Ganga in your matted hair!

O! Kapali! O! Creator of bliss! Who makes the minds of the good blossom!

Who has trusted in you and gone astray?

Only when it is realised that everything (material) is useless, does one feel the presence of God.

Every human will reach this state, it is certain. This should not be forgotten.

When the final hour comes the holy name of Siva may not rise in the tongue.

Hence O! Mind! start chanting a few names of Siva from today with love.

राग : मध्यमावती Rāga : Madhyamāvati

10. कर्पगमे – कडैक्कण् पाराय् (कर्पगमे)

चिर्परयोगियर् सिद्धर्गळ् ज्ञानियर्
तिरुवुडै अडियवर करुदुं वरमुदवुम्
तिरुमगळुं कलैमगळुं परवु तिरुमयिलैक् (कर्पगमे)

Kaṛpagamé - kaḍaikkaṇ pārāi (Kaṛpagamé)

Chiṛpara yogiyar siddhargal gnāniyar
Tiruvudai adiyavar karudun varamudavum
Tirumagaḷum kalaimagaḷum paravu tirumayilaik
(Kaṛpagamé)

सत्तु चिदानन्दमदाय् सकल उयिर्क्कुयिरायवळ् नी
तत्तुव मस्यादि महावाक्य तत्पर वस्तुवुं नी
सत्तुव गुणमोडु भक्ति शेर्प्पवर् भव
तापमुं पापमुं अऱ् इम्मैयिल् वर
सन्तान सौभाग्य संपत्
तोडु मरुमैयिल् निरतिशय इन्बमुं तरुम् (कर्पगमे)

Sattu chidānandamadāi sakala uyirkkuyirāyavaḷ nī
Tattuva masyādi mahāvākya tatpara vastuvum nī
Sattuva guṇamóḍu bhakti śerppavar bhava
Tāpamum pāpamum aṛa immaiyil vara
Santāna saubhāgya sampat
Tóḍu maṛumaiyil niratiśaya inbamum tarum (Kaṛpagamé)

10. Karpagame

O! Mother Karpaga! Please glance at me!

You grant the boons sought by your devotees, esteemed

Yogis, Siddhas and learned sages!

O! Mother Karpaga! Cast your glance on me.

You are praised by Lakshmi and Saraswati!

O! Mother Karpaga of Holy Mylai!

You are the life of all living beings as Existence, Consciousness and Bliss!

You are the crux of great sayings like: "Thou art that!"

O! Mother Karpaga! Bestow your glance on me!

You come to destroy the sins and sorrows of this birth of those of Sattvic quality who are devoted to you!

You bestow progeny, wealth and prosperity in this birth and unbelievable bliss in the life hereafter.

O! Mother Karpaga! Kindly cast your glance on me!